Bustin' Outta Brooklyn

Francis Chester-Cestari

Cestari Sheep & Wool Co.

Augusta Springs, Virginia

Bustin' Outta Brooklyn

Copyright © 2011 by 2011 by Francis Chester-Cestari

All rights reserved. No part of this book may be used or reproduced by any means, graphic, electronic, or mechanical, including photocopying, recording, taping or by any information storage retrieval system without the written permission of the publisher except in the case of brief quotations embodied in critical articles and reviews.

Cestari books may be ordered through booksellers or by contacting:

Cestari Sheep & Wool Co.
PO Box 10
Augusta Springs, VA 24411
www.CestariSheep.com
(540) 997-1212

ISBN: 979-8-218-16001-2

Printed in the United States of America

Cestari rev. date 5/1/2022

Dedication

It seems that when authors write books, they acknowledge their efforts to someone who influenced them while writing. This written undertaking is no exception.

Thus, I dedicate this book to the chief sources who have played overwhelming influences in my life. First, to God, who from the first day of my conception has played a constant role in everything I have achieved. Without Him I would be nothing.

So with deep humility, I thank Him for my family and blessing me with special parents. My father, Francesco Cestari (Frank), my personal hero, was always there for me with cogent advice and resources when needed. And my mom, Mary-Maria DeFrancesco Antonio, made sure I grew up healthy and focused on my studies.

And I offer further thanks for giving me a loving spouse, Diane, who loves our rural way of life and who has always been vocal about my ideas, supportive when needed, and for giving me four wonderful children. They are: Francis Scott Cestari, the best son a father could ever have; Angelique, a beautiful daughter who passed away at age twenty-eight; Jennifer Grimm, a spunky and sharp individual with great talents; and Sabrina Noele Chester, the laid back, multi-talented young woman who can be and do anything she puts her heart to.

I also thank God for my four beautiful grandchildren: Caleb, Ethan, Tristan Francis, and India Rose.

And I thank my cousin Christopher Chester for all his research on our family tree.

Also, with regards to the first printing and with utmost gratitude, I thank my Chief Editor, Kathleen Sampson, a resident of our community and former Public Affairs Representative for the U. S. Navy. She contributed many long hours of her professional expertise in editing this book and making it happen for me. As well, I extend thanks to my secretary, LCDR Charlotte B. Broga, U. S. Coast Guard (Ret.), who assisted in proofreading and administrative issues. She has since passed away.

      With regards to the second printing, most of the material in the first printing is incorporated in this printing, thus I sincerely thank Theresa Rosenthal, my wonderful social network director, for reviving my manuscript so that this book could be printed again.

      To all of these resources, my prayerful thanks, for it could not have been accomplished without the love and support from each of you.

Contents

1. Some History About Breaking Out

2. Learning the Ropes

3. Early Days of the Cestari Family

4. My Italian History

5. Role Models

6. The Family in World War II

7. Francis - With An "i"

8. Serving and Surviving

9. Those Wonderful, Unpredictable Nuns

10. Bishop Loughlin High School

11. College, Politics, and Goats

12. Mail Call

13. Dancing With the Holy Ghost

14. Wearing More Than One Hat

15. Bucking the Current at Law School

16. Farm Stand = Tuition

17. Lessons Learned

18. A Shepherd Meets His Mate

19. Wanting to Cotton to Virginia

20. The Yarn Business

21. The Wool Fair

22. Commonwealth of Virginia vs. Alex Poindexter

23. Have Sheep - Will Travel

24. A Shepherd Leads and Protects

25. Sheep Taking a Bow

26. Wool Mill # 1

27. My Life as a Professor

28. More Interesting Cases

29. Wool Mill #2

30. Shepherds' Remedies

31. Government Subsidies

32. Evil Thrives When Good Men Do Nothing - Lord Edmond Burke, M.P England 1729-1797

33. The Death Penalty

34. My Bitch with the Legal System

35. Grandparents as Substitute Parents

36. Mental Illness

37. Apologia

38. Personal Experiences with the Sacraments

39. In Defense of God

40. Assessments in Augusta County

41. Our Four Children

42. Keeping On

Preface

Brooklyn to me is both a physical place located in the westernmost part of Long Island with access to Manhattan and also a mental place of confinement and servitude, the antithesis of freedom.

Many people in life experience a time of being Brooklynized - that is, stuck either in physical or mental subjugation. It can be an association with a job you have, or a relationship or possibly an addiction that keeps you in servitude. It is a place that prevents you from being a God- created, free human being.

Many times it is very difficult to bust out of a Brooklynized situation, but as this book will disclose, it is never impossible. Difficult yes, but it's never impossible. I truly believe that all people should never have to endure a mental Brooklyn in their lives. The physical place known as Brooklyn, New York, had and continues to have special, wonderful characteristics and charms about it. It is close to the financial, publishing, fashion, and banking centers of America,

Brooklyn Botanical Gardens, libraries, parks, zoos, Eastern Parkway, and Coney Island, a revival of charming residences and sites of the Statue of Liberty and East River. Gone forever are Ebbits Field and other wonderful things such as farms. Yes, at one time Brooklyn was a great agricultural resource. However, it was and will never be for me. I could never be a free me in Brooklyn, and so the physical place called Brooklyn also took on a mentally constrictive place called Brooklyn.

If you have a Brooklyn in your life, be it the physical place called Brooklyn or the mental variety, and it has proven to be stifling, join me as we bust out of Brooklyn. I did, and never regretted it.

Chapter 1

Some History About Breaking Out

As a very young boy growing up in the eastern part of an undeveloped part of Brooklyn, I saw goats grazing on the Brooklyn meadow lands and vegetable farms and wanted so much to have my own animals. My father was an animal lover, not my mother.

I would bring home stray dogs and cats, and my mother would tell me that I couldn't have animals in Brooklyn. But I would show my mother all the goats grazing two or more blocks from her house. These stray animals would disappear as fast as I brought them home.

"No animals. Period," she said.

I would cry myself to sleep, and when I woke up the next morning, the stray animal was no longer with me.

I remember getting a black duckling for Easter from my godmother. It wasn't long until the little creature died. I made a coffin for that lovely animal and buried her. I never found out why she died. It was very hurtful to have to live in this environment and I blamed Brooklyn for my sadness in not being able to have animals. So breaking out of Brooklyn seemed to be the only way out of this mess and so I kept the faith and the hope that I would someday be free to have and love all the animals I wanted.

There was a beautiful library near my mother's home. (I never considered 185 Crystal Street as my home… my mother was the one who bought this detached home in the early 1930's before she was married. She always reminded Dad of that fact.) I would go to that library almost every day after school and read all the books they had on farm animals and gardens. I remember one book; I think it was called *Five Acres and Freedom*. I drooled over that book. It told about vegetables, blackberries goats and chickens and I would say to myself: *If only I had the money to buy five acres, just think of what I could do.*

I was determined to be a farmer. No one, especially my mother, was going to stop me in my efforts. Finally, she gave me permission to buy some chickens and I set them up in her backyard. When the eggs came, I sold them to the neighbors. And then the chickens began to die, one after the other.

I was told, "It must be the bad Brooklyn dirt."

Years later, a neighbor confessed to me that he poisoned all my chickens. Can you blame me for wanting to break out of Brooklyn? Not a single animal that I managed to get ever lived long at that house.

In the summer of 1946, my folks leased a lovely farm home in Huntington Station, Long island - on the North Shore of Suffolk, Long Island. The owner had a huge garden, well over a half an acre and he told me that I could have the garden. I can still feel the sensation of those words. It was truly the beginnings of breaking out of Brooklyn! My dad was so happy for me and he taught me all about raising vegetables. Then I made my move to expand things.

*Could I have some goats and chickens like my Grandma and Grandpa Cestari?" I pleaded. "We aren't in Brooklyn anymore," I pointed out. My dad brought me back to earth by reminding me that at the end of the summer I would have to give up the animals. Yes, and return to school and to Brooklyn.

I agreed to the reality of the situation. My father and I approached two Italian farmers, not far from the summer farm, who raised chickens and goats. We came home with two goats and two dozen laying hens. I was in heaven! At the age of ten, I was now a *real* farmer.

One Italian farmer gave me this advice: "Francesco, see here this is where the milk comes from…see here, this is the goat's mouth… food here makes milk here," he said in his wonderful Italian dialect. The farmers became wonderful friends. And all the eggs they gathered were taken in their trucks and sold - in Brooklyn! And they agreed to take back the animals at the end of the summer.

My dad taught me so much about the garden and the animals. I am eternally grateful for that man. He was so much a part of my dream to be a farmer. He was a strong counter punch to my anti-farmer mother.

Marketing was the next step. "How do we go about selling the produce from the farm?" I asked Dad.

"Francis, there are two ways. One, give it to a broker to sell and make next to nothing; or two, take it to the homes of the people and make good money," he said.

I elected to go with the second choice and loaded up my red wagon and started out. Loaded with all kinds of vegetables, milk, and eggs, I knocked on the screen door of the first house I came to. An unsmiling, angry and disheveled looking woman with a cigarette hanging from her lips came to the door. "What do you want?" I told her about my beautiful products. "Go away! You're bothering me with your junk!" she yelled and slammed the door in my face.

Tears came quickly. My image of grandeur was slipping and I was crushed. I slowly returned to my wagon, and a voice came to me and said: *Francis, don't give up. Go to the next house.* To this day, I truly believe that it was my guardian angel speaking to me. Was I going to respond positively to that voice, risking another blow to my then delicate morale or take the safe course and go home and give up on my dream of ever being a farmer?

I took a deep breath, and went to the next house. Carefully, this time, I knocked on the door and to my wonderful surprise was greeted by an absolutely lovely lady. Again, trying to spur myself back to my original enthusiasm, I told her I was learning to be a farmer and selling vegetables and eggs from my garden because I wanted to someday buy a five-acre farm of my own.

She came out of her house and to my wagon. "Why those vegetables are beautiful! You mean you raised these in your garden? Your chickens laid these eggs?"

"Yes ma'am!" I smiled.

"And I will take everything on the wagon," she said.

I walked away with a pocket full of money and a gigantic boost to my dream. Looking back, I think this woman was the most beautiful woman in the world. She is the reason that Chester Farms was created and later known by the Italian version, Cestari. I know that woman must be in heaven now and I am thankful that I listened to a voice much wiser than my own and had the determination to take action on it. Thank you lovely lady!

That was only the beginning.

Chapter 2

Learning the Ropes

The following year my folks rented another splendid house in Centerport, Long Island, also on the North Shore.

I was eleven years old then and earned money by cutting grass for the neighbors, and saved it to buy that farm of my own. So I started a little newspaper and called it *The New York Editorial*, and bought a little hand-printing machine and wrote stories, mostly about polio victims who were victimized by the disease. I secured statistics from the government and started selling the papers. I made friends with a young boy who agreed to work with me and we sold lots of papers because of the polio stories. And yes, I made a little money doing that, too.

My dad was pleased with my enthusiasm, and received permission from the manager of the *Long Island Press,* a major area newspaper at the time, for me to tour its offices, pressroom, and printing site. What an exciting evening it was to see the Linotype presses running. One of the operators even typeset my name on a metal matrix and gave it to me.

My heart was still with farming and so when a piece of land across from our rented summer home in Centerport was for sale, I pleaded with Dad to buy it. And he did. It was wooded, and just a quarter of an acre. He and I cleared that land and made it into a "farm" where I could put my goats and chickens.

A neighbor built a little closed-in shed with materials I gathered from the local dump. We made a concrete floor in it and built a chicken house. I was in heaven. In time. I had a crop of string beans ready to pick, and placed empty baskets among the rows to return the next day to fill them.

At sunrise, I crossed the road to my little farm only to find the entire crop of beans obliterated by a marauding animal. I was disheartened and confused, and felt just plain awful. The next morning my dad brought me the enemies, a pair of dead rabbits.

"How did you kill them?" I asked.

He showed me the method used in Italy by shepherds. Using a cord rope, he situated a rock in the middle of it, swung it around and with a flick of his wrist pulled back at a precise moment for the rock to fly at the target. "This is how shepherds in Italy defended the sheep that were being attacked by wolves and dogs," he said.

Summer came to an end and I dreaded having to give up my animals and return to Brooklyn. I conned my parents into allowing me to keep the animals over the winter and spring. I suggested that they could bring me back to the farm on Fridays and I could sleep in the small shed, and be a farmer over the weekend. I would return the goats to the neighboring farm, but set up automatic feeders for the chickens.

This worked out fine until my folks came to check on me one Saturday morning, opened the door to the shed and found me sleeping on the cot with a large garter snake coiled up next to me, also sound asleep. It didn't bother me; I knew they were not poisonous, so why worry.

Well, my mother thought otherwise. Besides, she said the chickens were eating all the grain the first two days of the week and starving until I arrived on Friday, so my overnight experiment with farming came to a crashing end. It was back to Brooklyn until the next summer.

Maybe it was the summer home, and maybe it was my passion for farming that matched his, but soon after, my father attempted to get my mother to move from Brooklyn. He sold the Centerport property and bought a small house on one and a half acres in Dix Hills, Long Island.

Dad and I worked the land, built chicken and goat houses and off I was with a real farm. When I was fourteen or fifteen Dad bought some land on Powerhouse Road in Roslyn Heights, Long Island to set up a garden center. With his permission I set up a fruit stand to sell produce, no more door to door.

He gave me the go ahead, and things were coming together. The fruit stand was an absolute success. At the age of sixteen, I hired my first, second, and third employees.

The first worker was captain of the local high school football team and what a marketing move that was! All the girls came with their moms to buy Chester Farms' products and of course converse and make eyes with my employee.

When it came time for me to get a Social Security number, I didn't mind paying taxes, but I learned real early that I did not want to take anything from the government and so I didn't get a number until I was eighteen. When I did, it was at the firm recommendation of my dad.

About then I learned about employees who steal. I was doing a land office business, and was suddenly losing money. Dad hid behind an old shed and saw an older female employee taking twenty dollar bills for herself. Later I too saw her in the act.

Again, with my father's strong recommendation and advice, we quietly discharged her, not telling her the reason. "I think we should let your mom take command of the farm stand," suggested my dad.

What? My non-farm mom?

And so it was. She loved the admiration she received from the people who drove up to the stand. Many of the locals loved that she could speak to them in Italian. Soon there were notables such as Perry Como, Kenny Gardner, Guy Lombardo, and more. Here was a woman with a second grade education drawing in the crowds with her sparkling personality and non-stop humor. The profits rolled in.

In the fifties, my stand was the place to go. I sold unbelievable amounts of food from my garden. I was able to get sweet corn from a farmer friend and also from a real farmers' "wholesale only" market in Huntington, Long Island operated by a northeastern farmers' cooperative because Long Island had farms, farms, and more farms! I paid Mom five dollars a day and she spent that on preparing food for Dad, my uncle Val, and me. That was my mom.

Once when I was a buyer at the marker I saw a Polish farmer come in with a load of fairly ripe tomatoes. He didn't speak much English, and I noticed that some buyers were getting together to steal his tomatoes with one buyer making one bid. I approached them. "That is wrong."

"He's ignorant, can't speak English, and so what?"

"So *what*... so *what*?" I bellowed. "It's wrong and I'm not going to let you guys get away with this." I stepped up and bid against them.

Somehow I wound up with one great big load of ripe tomatoes. But made my point. Thereafter there was no more stealing from the farmers, at least when I was there. I loaded the lot of tomatoes onto my truck. It was Friday with the weekend ahead. As I pulled in with my load, my mother took one look at the ripe tomatoes. "How in God's name do you expect to sell that load? What came over you to buy that?" she asked. I told her my story.

"Good luck," she said. All she could see was good money and lots of ripe tomatoes going to the dump.

It was after some thought that we had a "sale." There were lots of takers, and lo and behold we sold every last one of the tomatoes by Sunday night. "Now that was a miracle," Mom sighed.

During the time I had my farm stand I realized that I needed to have fresh Long Island corn by July Fourth, an almost impossible task at the time. I looked at the map of Long Island and saw a possibility and so I called our agricultural extension agent. I learned that there was a young Cornell College graduate living near Orient Point on Long Island. I contacted him and discovered he was able to get fresh corn by July first or earlier because of the warm current near his farm. He was shipping the corn by ferry to Boston. I decided to work a deal with him, and so I would leave for his farm at four thirty or five o'clock in the morning and be the first one there to have the sweet corn. My farm stand had sweet corn for two weeks before anyone else.

I also went to New York City's Old Washington Market on the southwest side of Manhattan to purchase fresh California and Washington State fruit. They also had fresh peaches, first out of Georgia and up the coast as it became warmer. It was exciting to walk through this wholesale market at night and smell the freshness of all the products.

When I first went to that market with my truck I realized that it was owned by Italians and Jews who work together really well. Each produce broker is an independent operation. All the brokers were kind to me and taught me the ropes.

One night - the market was only open at night - I noticed that peaches were priced very high. One broker knowing me to be a young inexperienced buyer, told me to wait about an hour and the price would most certainly go down. He demonstrated how the system worked.

The brokers were in contact with the farmers and when the prices were low, they would have them pull off the road for coffee and advise them when the prices rose. They would later direct the farmers into Manhattan so they could gain the greater cost.

It was sad for me to see poor people in the old tenements sleeping or sitting on the fire escapes. It was easy to hear, see and smell the conditions of poverty. I asked my dad why would anyone want to live in such an environment, when in just a few miles in any direction from Brooklyn, Bronx, or Manhattan lies a beautiful rural countryside.

"It is lack of knowledge and education, and sometimes lack of motivation that prevented them from improving," he said.

I can still see the beauty of the market and the drudgery of poverty, side by side.

Still now, I contemplate the issue of poverty and have concluded that there are really two types of poverty. They are often people who cannot care for themselves due to physical illness, injury or severe mental disability, and second, people who are indigent due to alcohol and drug abuse, laziness and lack of motivation.

The second group needs to be motivated without society acting as enablers. I don't think we should allow their children to suffer for the sins of their parents. St. Paul said it well two thousand years ago, and Captain John Smith four hundred years ago, "... he who is lazy, let him starve."

One of the seven capital sins is sloth, otherwise known as laziness. Society should not be beholden to lazy people. It is unjust to society that the workers give to the sloth-loving people.

Chapter 3

Early Days of the Cestari Family

The Cestari family has lived for centuries in Basilicata Province in south central Italy. Family members have resided in and around a little village known as Marsico Nuovo, near Potenza. Sheep abound in this most rural part of Italy and their sheep grazed on the grounds of a monastery high in the mountains of Italy.

There, it was tradition to list the father's occupation on his child's birth certificate. Cestari children customarily had the word pastore (shepherd), or *farmer*, cited on theirs. Records of this tradition go back three hundred years. Interestingly, the word pastor comes from pastore, meaning shepherd or leader.

My paternal grandfather, Carmine Cestari, came to America in 1902 to explore its economic possibilities. Three years later, my grandmother, Angelina, and their three sons, John and Francesco (my father), Dominic and their sister, Anna, followed. Carmine was encouraged to do this after one of my great uncles came to the United States and wrote him about its wonders. Carmine landed at Ellis Island, off Manhattan, took one look at New York City, and being a shepherd, said to himself: *I'm heading to the country.*

And that country was Roslyn, Long Island, on the North Shore. He gained permission to live on the property of a sand and gravel company located on the banks of Hempstead Harbor owned by the Pope family. There, he put together abandoned materials and built himself a shack where he, his wife and four children, Anna, John, Dominic, and my father, Francesco (Frank) would live temporarily. Eventually, the number of children grew to ten, all of whom survived to adult ages.

They had a garden, pigs, goats, chickens, and an assortment of other animals that supplied them with the daily necessaries plus fish for

Friday dinners. (Catholics were not permitted to eat meat on Fridays in reverence to Christ's death on the cross on Good Friday. In recent years, that rule was rescinded but today, our family continues that tradition.)

Grandfather Cestari secured employment with the New York Central Railroad in upstate New York laying track for the company. He was paid ninety cents per day, with ten cents of that taken for payment to the straw boss, or one who did the hiring.

My father and his siblings attended a one-room schoolhouse for grades one through eight that had only one teacher. My father told me that he learned much in this environment because the teacher would teach one grade at a time giving the other grades the opportunity to learn, or review, other lessons. School began each morning with the Pledge of Allegiance to the flag and the *Our Father*. He was also an altar boy at Saint Mary's Catholic Church in Roslyn and told me that he had to get there by rowboat.

My grandparents later moved to the adjacent community of Port Washington. Even with such a large family they purchased property that had a house, and a general store, which the family operated. They would eventually own several rental homes, an auto garage, gas station, and second general store combined. My father and his five brothers worked in the auto garage, which served as a gas station, auto repair shop, towing service, and even sold new Cord and Hupmobile cars. Later, they owned and operated three auto stations.

Their success begs the question as to how immigrant parents with minimal education and ten children to rear were able to accumulate all this. Family history says it was the matriarch of the family - Grandma Angelina Cestari and her pot on top of the icebox. As each member of the family was paid for a job, they and Grandpa would put all of the earnings into that pot and Grandma Cestari saw to paying for the needs of the family.

There was no such thing as anyone out for him or herself in that house. In an Italian family, there is no such thing as "mine," it's the family's, period. This can have remarkable good consequences for the capital growth of a family. It did just that for my father's family.

With a system like Grandma Cestari's, wealth grows rapidly. Of course it takes putting the family ahead of self to accomplish such a result. Bottom line: each child inherited a piece of real estate or the equivalent in cash. Yes, the principle of one for all and all for one works. And yet their community did not seem to feel the same way.

Back in those days, many Americans did not like Italians. Possibly, those in the US saw them only as poor and unable to speak English Italians were, however, devoted to their Catholic faith, their families and extremely ambitious and passionate about life.

The non-Italians in my grandparents' community would not even say their name Cestari with its true pronunciation, but instead would call them Chester. To non-Italian ears, Cestari sounded like Chester and so the name Chester was used interchangeably with Cestari.

My mom was born in Naples, Italy, and was the eldest of nine living children. Her parents were Margaret and Enrico DeFrancesco Antonio, As a young girl, my grandmother, Margaret, lived in Compania, on an olive operation where the olives were pressed and exported.

My grandfather Enrico was from Naples and met my grandmother under unusual circumstances. As he was traveling around Campania on his horse, he couldn't take his eyes off Margaret Bruno, a woman of extraordinary beauty who worked at her parents' olive business. She had long curly dark black hair, beautiful skin and piercing eyes.

Enrico, tall and very dashing, was immediately taken by Margaret's beauty. They talked and it was then and there he decided that Margaret was for him. Period. And Margaret did like this charming man riding his horse. Soon afterwards, he took off with his willing beauty and married against Margaret's family's wishes. The Brunos pursued Enrico with a vengeance.

My grandparents headed for Naples for several months keeping ahead of the Bruno family who pursued them. By then, Margaret was pregnant, and Enrico booked passage on a ship going to Argentina.

Argentina was a major attraction to Italians emigrating from Italy and looking for their fortune. Today, a little less than half the population in Argentina is of Italian extraction.

Just as my grandparents started to board the ship, my grandmother went into labor and was ordered off the ship by its captain. As it would be, Margaret gave birth to my mother, Maria. They remained in Italy just long enough to take the next boat from Naples. Its destination was for the United States.

I think how close I came to becoming an Argentinean! It was a fascinating series of events. A horse brought my grandparents together and many years later it was because of a horse that I met Diane.

Chapter 4

My Italian History

Francesco Cestari

My dad was born in a small Italian village in Marselo Nuovo, near Potenza in the province of Basilicata. His parents Carmine and Angelina were quite poor being subsistence farmers grazing sheep on the monastery grounds high in the mountains. There would be ten children in their family.

Basilicata is one of the most rural provinces in Italy. Basil, the herb, abounds there, along with sheep. It adjoins Compania province where Naples is located and where my mom was born.

Carmine and Angelina took the children by boat to St. Mary's Catholic Church in Roslyn Harbor. My father was an altar boy who regularly served at mass. I should add that Italians tend to be Catholic. In Italy, ninety-nine percent are, although many do not attend mass regularly. Catholicism and the Italian nationality are inseparable. It is part and parcel of their heritage.

In a few years, that family accumulated sufficient capital to go into the nearest town, Port Washington, Long Island, and purchase a house with a building that could be used as a general store.

My father, upon graduation from the eighth grade, went to work on the Hicks Estate along the Long Island Sound. He was a gardener and later a chauffeur for Congressman Hicks. The Hicks family traced their lineage to early Dutch settlers on Long Island and was very wealthy. Through his employment with the congressman, he met Presidents Warren Harding and Calvin Coolidge. What an education he obtained!

The family continued to grow economically being in business for themselves. The children, even though initially having outside jobs, still contributed to Angelina's money pot. In short order they bought houses, which they rented out and finally a fine home on Port Washington Boulevard, the main road to town and the luxury estates along Sands Point. When my grandparents died, their estate was divided amongst the children. No arguments, just working things out together.

My father was a short man, being only five feet tall but built like a rock, and strong as a lion. He was a member of the Knights of Columbus, a Catholic fraternity, and represented the Knights as an amateur boxer, winning many bouts.

"How did you handle men who are taller than you?" I asked.

"I would work them hard on the inside so that they could never maximize their asset to throw long powerful punches," he explained.

Sometimes people made fun of my father and although he never, it seemed, took it to heart. It angered me that people would hurt other people, especially my dad. Words hurt more than punches. I grew up never wanting to make fun of anyone with a disability. I would always interfere and admonish my fellow students when this happened. It is cruel and wrong and it always bothered me when this happened as it caused me to recall my dad's suffering.

He was my hero and I saw him as a giant of a man. He was a quiet man, atypical of Italians, which was the Cestari trait, quiet and humble but very joyful and thankful for being alive. I am sure their humble roots made them such a remarkable people.

One negative with that side of my family is an un-Italian trait, and that is that they were not overly affectionate. When I was a little boy I would hunger for my dad's physical affection, but it was not there. I remember going to my mom who was just the opposite, affectionate at the drop of a hat, and telling her, "Dad doesn't love me; he never shows affection to me."

My mom grabbed me and told me that my dad's family had my, difficult times and lacked physical display of affection. "You are the apple of your father's eye and he loves you dearly," she assured me.

I remember just one time he opened up with outward affection. We had just been to a movie and he held my hand and sang to me.

You are my sunshine.
My only sunshine.

You make me happy when skies are grey.
You'll never know dear how much I love you.
Please don't take my sunshine away.

It took some time for me to understand that, but my father showed his love in many ways, small and large. When I won a scholarship to Bishop Loughlin Memorial High School in Brooklyn, he was able to help me with my studies up to and including algebra. For science class, he helped me set up a live tree propagation system for which I won an award *and* received an A for the class.

A particular memory is from 1963. I was being admitted to practice before the United States Supreme Court in Washington, DC. Just as soon as he finished his work, Dad drove that night from Brooklyn over winding roads, as Interstate 95 was in the process of being built, to the hotel where I was staying. He arrived late, and there were no available rooms at the hotel where I was staying. Instead of waking me, he was permitted to sleep on the couch in the lobby. My dad was there for my induction, a great effort on his part.

There were many other acts of kindness too. I remember the lunches and talks we had each day. Even with all the education I had --twenty-two years worth--I always considered my father as my mentor and intellectually superior to me. He was truly my hero and the wisest man I have ever known.

Maria Cestari

After her parent's wild escape from her mother's family and nearly moving to Argentina, Mom was their first born of nine in San Giuseppe, a village near Naples, Italy.

Quite different from Dad's family, Mom's father, Enrico, came from an educated, wealthy background. When her parents came to America bringing their little Maria, they too arrived at Ellis Island and settled in a less populated section on the eastern part of Brooklyn.

Grandfather Enrico was a gambler. One day he was rich, the next day,he had nothing. The family had unsettling economic situations. He owned a garment factory employing sixty-five people and the next day he was working for the new winners of the plant. He was the first in

his area to buy an automobile, and the first to lose one. Women loved him. He was a charmer, and despite all of his failings, Maggie (as she was called) loved her Enrico. In her mind, he could do no wrong. Years later when he died, they had nothing in material goods to leave to his children; a seemingly wasted life. Despite his self-centered behavior, to his credit, he was an excellent dresser with superb manners and all of his children turned out well.

With unstable conditions at home, my mom, being the eldest, was forced to leave the second grade. At the age of seven, she went to work at a garment factory. She soon became a pattern maker, creating the standards for the production workers, earning the most of all the staff. She, like my father, was an unbelievable worker. Having a father as a gambler, Mom was determined to have a stable home. She worked in her basement operating a non-electric sewing machine making patterns tor that local garment plant. A haggler over prices, she was a saver and a penny pincher who became a reasonably wealthy woman of her time.

At one point, Grandfather Enrico even gambled away his home and the family was about to be dispossessed. Because her father took her earnings, my mom secretly was able to save money from pay raises that she didn't tell him about. When she was twenty-three, Mom bought a lovely home at 185 Crystal Street, located at the edge of Brooklyn's "civilization". There were meadows, and views as far as the bay. Grandfather Enrico was furious at her for holding back her earnings and slapped her. But he gladly took residence in her house.

Despite her experiences, Mom was one of the most fun loving persons I knew, and she loved to laugh. Jokes and jovial stories abounded from her mouth.

A favorite story was actually about how her father treated her so poorly. "Once I desperately needed shoes, and my father bought me a pair that was very oversized and *used*. One day I was crossing a street when a bicycle ran over my shoes, turning them up at the ends, just missing my toes!" she related. "When I complained about it, my father said, "See! I saved you from injury because of the shoes I got you." Her manner and gestures in the telling would have people howling with laughter.

My mom wanted so much for me to be somebody "great." She insisted that I eat healthy foods and would massage my legs fearing that I would be short. Dad, on the other hand, wished for me to be secure with a backup profession to complement my love of farming. I chose the profession of law as I thought it would least interfere with my "practice of farming and shepherding." They were both so instrumental in the paths I would take.

Chapter 5

Role Models

Mary and Francesco

My parents, Mary and Francesco, met at a funeral. My mother's best friend was Elma Senatore. Elma's mother arranged for my folks' parents to be introduced to each other. Thus, the idea of "my son and your daughter" came to the forefront, and a wonderful marriage was born. My mother was about seven inches taller than my father, and they did not appear as a traditional couple. However, their love overcame society's expectations. They married within a year after their first meeting. There is something positive about arranged marriages as so many of them seemed to prove successful.

Dad was in love with my mom from the first time he saw her. Not so with her. She told me that she didn't feel love for my father at first but she cared for him. "He was so kind and such a good man. I learned to love him," she said. They never left each other, only death separated them.

Their marriage was met with the stresses of the Great Depression.which hit Long Island around 1934 or 1935. When the bank my father's family used closed its doors, along with family's funds on deposit, my father and his brothers decided the business could not support six families. Since my father did not yet have children to support, he voluntarily withdrew from the family business without taking a penny.

Starting out with an old car, a push lawn mower, shovel and rake, he began building a landscaping business. When he died in 1967, he had a fine, debt-free company with ten employees and the business property.

Before my parents met, my mother bought a house in Brooklyn for five thousand dollars, which was a high price during the Depression, and within one hundred feet of it sat an estate with beautiful grounds. I call it my mother's home because she paid for it and was so in love with that special place in her life. The house became our family home.

Dad then started a landscaping business with an old car, a pick, shovel, hand mower, and clippers. His seven-day work week brought in eighteen dollars. My mother added to their income by working from home in the cellar making patterns for a dress company on a hand-operated sewing machine. Their work ethic always seemed to keep some money coming in.

They wanted a family, and when my mother had difficulty conceiving a child, my mom went to a convent. "Will you pray for me and Frank to have a baby?" she asked the nuns.

On the convent grounds was a beautiful statue of Saint Francis of Assisi. As she stood there admiring it, my mom invoked the prayers of this saint who was also my dad's namesake (Francesco). "I promise to name any child Francis," she prayed.

And so I was named Francis.

"Francis," she began, "please tell me you will always use your full given name in honor of the promise I made to St. Francis." I have honored her request.

When I was born, Elma's sister came to my mother's hospital room, held me up and said, "This day a farmer has been born. All he needs is a pair of overalls."

That was not my mother's vision for her baby's life. She raised her voice. "He is not going to be a farmer! He is going to be someone whom people can look up to!" She did all she could to ensure I did not become a farmer.

She was also adamant to keep me as healthy as possible, Mom fed me cod liver oil every day. She massaged my legs so they wouldn't be short, and saw to it that I ate the healthiest foods possible, such as goat's milk and cheese, and used olive oil in her cooking. No junk food or deep-fried food for me. Exercise was also a daily routine.

With this regimen I had an over abundance of energy. Often when away from home, Mom used a harness made for children to keep me under control. Once we passed a ditch digger working on the new subway. I was going every which way but forward, and he told my mother not to worry about having other children as "one like him you will never have again".

Although born in Brooklyn, I was blessed to live in what were then the outskirts of Brooklyn where homes were rustic, goats grazed, and vegetable gardens were abundant. Yes, there were farms in Brooklyn during mid-Twentieth Century. By virtue of my father's landscaping business on the North Shore of Long Island, I saw and visited farms weekly and loved going with him to Long Island.

My Cestari grandparents had a relatively small subsistence farm and general store with lots of chickens, goats, pigs, fruits, vegetables and flowers, just what one would expect from an Italian family. Much to my mom's dismay, it only fueled my love of animals and outdoor life.

Elma Jenatore -- godmother and second mom

And what happened to my mother's friend, Elma, who engineered the meeting of my parents? Aunt Elma, as I would call her, was my mother's maid of honor at my parents' wedding. Later in her life, she married and acquired the last name of Petrich, but did not have children of her own.

When Aunt Elma became my godmother, she was an active, hands-on and in-your-face godmother and a major figure in my life. My mom said, in admiration, "Elma is truly your second mother."

I loved her like a mom, too. More than anyone, this outstanding Christian woman taught me about the Catholic Church and instilled in me the love and passion I have for it. Aunt Elma would take me to church every Sunday and was always there for me in good times and bad. She believed in me, and in her eyes, I could do no wrong.

Of course, I made my share of mistakes, but Aunt Elma's guidance in faith and morals kept me pretty straight. It's difficult to do otherwise when someone who loves you also believes in you.

At the age of twelve, I received the sacrament of confirmation, which was administered by a bishop of the Roman Catholic Church. The sacrament is believed to give Catholics special strength from the Holy Spirit, and enable them to spread and defend their faith.

Aunt Elma wanted me to have a gift that was substantial and memorable for that big day. She rode a subway train to Manhattan and purchased a large, beautifully painted statue of the sacred heart of Jesus. Handmade and painted in Italy, it is a more-than three-foot tall sculpture of Jesus pointing to his exposed heart, declaring His love for mankind.

Aunt Elma carried this heavy statue on the train, through the subway station, and finally on the elevated train's last stop and to me at my home. She even had it blessed by a priest in our church. "Always keep it in a prominent place in your home as a reminder of God's love for you," Aunt Elma instructed. It is also a reminder of her love for me.

Now, more than sixty-three years old, the statue is in our dining room, and each morning I touch the top of it, thank God for another day, and ask for specific guidance. What a wonderful way to start my day.

Aunt Elma was a chip off the old block, and so much like her mom Rose Senatore, who, in my opinion, was an absolute saint. Mrs. Sentore's heart seemed to be filled with joy, and she was always doing something to help others. When the nuns had a project afloat for students to earn money for the Catholic school, Mrs. Sentore was there to help.

I would come home from school with candy or cards to sell, and my mother would say, "Don't go to Rose's house! She only buys these things because it's you selling them."

But I would go anyway. "Mrs. Sentore, my mother said I am bothering you with this."

"Don't listen to your mother! You come here anytime and I will help you with your sales," she said. Mrs. Sentore always had money to help out the good nuns.

This happy woman loved people and holidays and special family events where she played Italian music on her accordion and she would sing too. Religious books and articles were a favorite and she also had a vast collection of bibles. I treasure an English translation of the Latin Vulgate Bible that she gave me. It is now over one-hundred-sixty years old and I read it from time to time, and have had it rebound.

I was just nine years old on the day I visited Mrs. Sentore and found her in her bedroom. She took me to a window and said, "Look, Francis, what a wonderful rainbow."

I stood by the window, searching the sky. "But there's no rainbow there."

"Yes there is," she said. "And it is beautiful."

That night, Mrs. Sentore, in her early sixties, passed away in her sleep as peacefully as she lived. I was the last person to see her alive.

Because of my father, mother, Aunt Elma, and Mrs. Sentore, who were so much a part of my upbringing, I was able to achieve high standards by which to live. I feel such deep gratitude to have loved, and have been loved by, such extraordinary people.

Chapter 6

The Family in World War II

It was early that December Sunday morning in 1941. I was with my father at a newsstand when he bought a copy of The New York Daily News. The front page read "Japs Bomb Pearl Harbor," with a picture of the sinking of the battleship USS Arizona.

It was a little more than a month before my sixth birthday and I clearly remember that "day of infamy" and the days of World War II. It was a fascinating, but fearful time for children, or anyone, to be living.

My dad loved history as well as geography and I became interested in those subjects too. He and my Cestari uncles, except for two, were over the required age for military service. My Uncle Dominic owned and operated a Jersey dairy farm located in Cherry Valley, New York, near Cooperstown. Because farming was considered a vital industry for the war effort, and his active involvement in it, Uncle Dominic had a farm exemption from military service.

Uncle Valentine Cestari, or Valentine Chester, my father's youngest brother, was my godfather. Uncle Val was drafted in late 1942. He was trained in New York and Colorado to serve in the US Army Corps of Engineers' Tenth Mountain Division for the eventual battles in Italy. He fought his way through the Po River Valley and onto the Italian Alps where his outfit lost two thirds of its troops.

When he came home I asked him how come he survived without being hurt. "Thank God, I was not curious. I kept my head down when at times keeping your head down was a good idea," he said. He was a full sergeant with only a side arm for a weapon.

Uncle Val's job was to see that the fields ahead of the troops were prepared for the division to advance, to build bridges, and roads leading up and around mountains, with other necessary engineering tasks. The Division was routinely under front line attack by the German SS.

"Were the SS good soldiers?" I asked him.

"When you put a bullet in one of them, they fell over and died like any other soldier."

One particular story was about when he didn't keep his head down. Uncle Val's colonel asked him to retrieve a bulldozer that was in no man's land, a region under the control of neither side. This bulldozer was vital for his outfit to build the roads for the advancing US Army.

Uncle Val had one man drive him and another soldier in a Jeep to the site of the bulldozer. The driver of the Jeep then drove back to the American line. My uncle and his man did the necessaries to get the track back in place and my uncle got on the bulldozer and drove it back to his lines with his man.

When the SS realized what was going on they started a barrage of gunfire at the bulldozer. My uncle and his man made it back safely. Uncle Val earned a Bronze Star for that effort. What he and his men did took guts and that, together with our industrial might, won that war.

My mother had several brothers who were drafted. My youngest uncle, Louis DeFrancesco volunteered for the US Army at the age of seventeen. He was involved in the Italian campaign at the Anzio Beach landing some distance south of Rome, near Naples where my mother was born. Upon landing, he was seriously wounded. I remember seeing my grandparents and my mother cry when learning of Uncle Louie's serious wounds. He survived and was again shipped out to the front. Again he was wounded but this time returned to the States.

Uncle Louie was an adventurous soul and was one of the first to land at Anzio. Around this time and before, beginning with the landing at Sicily, the Italian defenders realized that many of the Americans invading Sicily were Italian Americans, some even Italian born. Our country put many of the Italian-Americans in that situation, and for the most part, the Italians refused to shoot those who could be their own kin. When the Germans realized this, the Nazis pulled many divisions of their troops from the western front into Italy to hold the line against the invading American and British armies. In the long run this was to be a prophetic event making the eventual landing at Normandy the following year much easier.

At Anzio the Germans brought in many of their tanks, scattered them around the area, and used them as artillery barrages against my Uncle Louie's outfit. A young boy, Luigi Retrosi, lived near the place where German tanks were firing at my uncle's outfit, and where my uncle was seriously wounded. Sixty-three years later, Luigi Retrosi is a member of my parish and remembered very well hearing about that landing in his home. How amazing life is.

History tells us that Mussolini had kept Italy out of the war until the fall of France in 1940 when he tied Italy to Germany as an axis ally. This proved to be a disastrous decision. First of all this was an incompatible alliance consisting of opposites in personalities and culture. The only reason for Italy to enter the war was Mussolini's desire to obtain additional land for his country and he saw with the quick defeat of France the chance with Hitler to gain territory. This alliance was water and oil, never to mix.

There were definitely effects of the war on my own immediate family. My mother was an air raid warden at a nearby school. Just about everything was rationed, sugar, olive oil, meat, gasoline, rubber tires, just to name a few. Ration stamps were issued and were necessary to purchase a desired product.

I remember taking my red wagon to the coal-rationing center to get our supply of coal for heat. I also remember how hard everyone worked. We too had a victory garden and raised all kinds of food including a huge grape arbor. My mother made delicious grape preserves each fall.

World War II proved to have a positive side for me. My father posted the world map on our kitchen curtain next to the breakfast table and would put pins at the approximate location where my family members were doing battle. I learned a lot of geography and history during World War II because my father made the subjects interesting and very personal.

Chapter 7

Francis - With An "i"

When it came time to attend school, the Catholic schools were overcrowded so I started kindergarten in public school where there actually was a vegetable farm next to the school. I was there until second grade and did not thrive at all.

I was full of energy and looked to cause problems, like tying the girls' braids together and other stupid antics. Finally I was brought to the principal's office. He called my mother. "Find another school for him," the principal told her. "We cannot keep Francis as a student here. Find another school, or ... he is headed elsewhere."

This created an emergency. Mom called Aunt Elma for help and my godmother quickly found a Catholic school that might consider taking me in. She and my mom took me to the school, and left me alone in the church to pray for my fate while they talked with the Mother Superior. I was just eight, afraid and sat quietly realizing that I had taken things too far. It seemed like hours until Sister came to the church for me with my mom and Aunt Elma.

Sister Alphonso spoke with me and hugged me. "Mrs. Chester, and Miss Sentore, I would like to welcome Francis as a student at St. Rita's School."

That was an earth-shaking change in my life. My mom and Aunt Elma smiled and we all hugged one another. And so began my long career with Catholic schools, which was to be completed twenty years later after grammar school, high school, college, law school and graduate school - all Catholic schools and I must say I loved almost every moment of it.

When I was first enrolled in St. Rita's Catholic School, my mother advised the teachers that I was always to be called Francis, not Frank or any other appellation; Francis was my name. Sister instructed the class to always call me Francis and she emphasized "Francis." Unfortunately, the students thought Francis was a girl's name although the spelling of the female version of the name is Frances.

So with this introduction, I had to battle my fellow students, and I do mean fight, to protect myself and to secure my proper name and its spelling. This was the kickoff for daily fights on my way home from school.

Mom dressed me to the hilt in a school where students came from poor Italian families. I would have to fight off as many as twenty kids in a day, arriving home with dirty, sometimes ripped, white shirts with blood on them from me or my attackers.

I refused to be called anything but Francis - with an "i."

Mary Soviero, who lived near the school, would come out with her broom and put it to work on these pugnacious characters who tried to beat me up. This was a daily routine for a couple of years. In the meantime, my father had taught me to defend myself and I can assure you that I never ran away. I fought my way home and left a measure of my efforts upon these rascals.

I was eventually accepted as one of them with my body, and my name - Francis with an "i" intact.

Chapter 8

Serving and Surviving

St. Rita's School opened up a whole new world for me, which included becoming an altar boy. Being one was, in my mind, a way to thank God for saving me from being expelled from public school, a fate I thought was worse than hell.

Serving at mass meant the world to me. After making my First Holy Communion, I was permitted to serve at mass. That included lighting the candles, assisting with the wine and wafers, standing on the altar with the priest in front of the congregation, and wearing a black cassock and white surplice. It was a humbling experience, yet filled me with an extraordinary feeling of joy. I liked it! It came to the point where I looked forward to serving more than one mass in a day, and then my wish came true.

On an exceptionally snowy day, I was scheduled to serve the six-thirty morning mass. Back then, St. Rita's had four priests and could have more than one mass a day.

The snow was deep, and the winds were gusting that morning. walked the three quarters of a mile to the church with my head lowered against the wind and trying to keep snow out of my boots. Once there, I discovered I was the only server and prepared the altar and served the mass. Several older Italian women, who lived next to the church and were regulars, sat close to the front.

Servers did not make it for the seven o'clock mass and I stayed and served once more, and again, the only server for the seven-thirty service. At eight o'clock, there was a requiem mass for a church member.

During each of those masses, I actually kept hoping that the ale boys wouldn't show up for the next. I wanted to continue my altar-boy marathon. It was then and there that I considered becoming a priest, and continued wondering about it until my senior year in high school.

I realized that God had another path in which I could be adventurous interesting, and serve him as an inspiration for others' hope, faith, and determination. It was also a time when I realized that girls were nice to have around!

Over my life, there have been hundreds of priests, nuns, brothers. bishops, and even two popes that I have personally known. Out of all of these people, only two I consider to have shown undesirable and scandalous behavior to the Catholic Church. None involved sex, and both were priests.

My first exposure to conduct unbecoming a priest was during the ten o'clock morning mass at St. Rita's. At the sermon, this priest started in with his usual fire and brimstone message after which, he would leave the altar and personally go to the aisle and collect money from parishioners).

During his sermon, I was the lone altar boy and sat along the wall not far from the priest on the opposite side of the altar. My chair would give off a slight creak every time I breathed. Breathe. Creeeeeek. Breathe. Creeeeek.

After about five minutes of the creaking sound, this priest took the large missal used for mass and tossed it towards me. It landed near the altar.

"Get off the altar!" he yelled.

Following his instructions, I genuflected in front of the tabernacle. exited to the sacristy off the altar and waited for the priest to finish his sermon. When he was through speaking to the congregation, I returned to the altar and continued serving mass. This priest never said anything to me afterwards.

However, when I opened the church door to leave, there was a large, angry crowd of people who had been at mass. "How could you continue serving that rotten man?" someone asked.

"I don't think of it that way. I wasn't serving him. I was serving God," I said.

They were quiet. "Let's not go after Father. Just pray,"I urged, adding as I left, "And call the bishop if you want to."

In just two months, Father "Missal Tosser" suddenly retired and was replaced by a wonderful priest.

The second priest was initially wonderful. At least wonderful for several years, as he reestablished the Altar Boy Society, Knights of Columbus Council, and Perpetual Adoration Chapel.

Father Wonderful later changed his demeanor. He became belligerent towards me and others, resulting in many people leaving the parish, and some even left the Catholic Church. This priest had me removed from serving as Extra-ordinary Eucharistic Minister, and other activities. It was clear he wanted me out of "his" parish.

It was a terrible spiritual time for me. I perceived this priest as mean spirited and lacking compassion. I felt and detested the anger I had toward that man. He hurt me so deeply and that feeling was compounded when I saw the results of his spiritual cruelty to others. I had to confess many times my anger in my heart.

Being an altar boy brought some benefits too. Even though I wanted to break out of Brooklyn to become a farmer, I also loved baseball. Mr. Walter O'Malley, owner of the Brooklyn Dodgers, and a good Irish Catholic, gave us altar boys free tickets for bleacher seats to a number of the Dodger games. This enjoyment of this special occasion was enhanced by a priest who provided transportation, and gave us treats at the park out of his own pocket. I loved those Brooklyn Dodgers, especially because the big shots looked down on them. They were a team with little talent but big hearts and they won, but never seemed to make it in the World Series. Every time they would lose the Series, we would all say, "Wait 'til next year!" And next year eventually did come.

In 1955, just before their move to Los Angeles, they won their first and only World Series against the big-shot Yankees. All of Brooklyn, along with Long Island, went crazy that day. Our beloved Dodgers showed the world that determination does the trick.

Chapter 9

Those Wonderful, Unpredictable Nuns

The School Sisters of Notre Dame taught classes at Saint Rita's Catholic School in Brooklyn. They kept things upbeat, and would play recordings of John Philip Souza's marches as we marched to exit the school. Sisters wore long black habits with starched white material around their head and upper chest. There was something fascinating, and yet mysterious, about the sisters and their habits.

Wearing habits set them apart from the general population. They stood out every time they were in public. Nuns were respected, and people would step aside when they walked by and the sisters would greet them with smiles and sensitivity. These ladies were special, and were respected at my school by the students, staff and priests. The priests would tell us that the nuns are special people, God's special people. They are also God's special friends.

Later, in high school, a religious brother told us that the world's culture and morals rises and falls at the direction of women. "If women set their standards high, men will rise to those high standards. If set low, men will be happy to accommodate women. When it comes to matters of human sexuality, women are the leaders and men the followers. Women have an awesome power to make the world a better place." he said.

I agree with that brother and also think that women are the greatest gift that God gave to the world. Every woman is a creation of beauty. If there were only men in the world, our world without women would self-destruct. Women bring class to the world; women bring culture to the world; and women bring morality to the world.

Things started to change academically for me in eighth grade. My mom was determined that I was going to be somebody. Every time I excelled in class on a test, or project, she would have a party at Sal's Italian Restaurant and invite the whole family and would extol my "virtues." It was embarrassing and I told her so, but it went on. Every A or award I received brought the family together at Sal's to congratulate me.

I realized later that she had a tough life and was always put down by her father who had the ability for greatness, but wasted his talents on gambling and women. My mom was determined that I was going to be somebody. It makes me wonder if I put my act together at that point because it meant so much to her. Here we have a woman with only a second grade education who wanted so much to exceed in life and was held down.

Overall, as a student I was never at the top of the class but was above average. The person who always led the class was Barbara Michele. She was pretty and smart. I had an eye for her but no reciprocity. Her dad was a leading medical doctor in the community and she and her family lived in a beautiful home. Her grandparents raised thoroughbred race horses in New Jersey, which increased the attraction.

The class was once assigned to write a story, pretending that we were reporters preparing an article for a newspaper. My piece was about a make-believe baseball game. After reading it, Sister called me over and told me I had a great ability for storytelling.

"The way you put a reader right into the action, you could very easily be a sports writer," she said.

This surprised the other sisters at the convent. With the exception of Mother Superior Alphonso, I was just a run-of-the mill sort of boy with a lot of talk and happy times. At the convent, Mother Superior was my greatest fan.

When it came time for selecting a high school, I wanted, and had my parents' blessing, to go to a Catholic high school. A scholarship was being offered at the diocesan school of Bishop Loughin High School at Green and Vanderbilt Avenues. At that time the area was decidedly a picturesque part of Brooklyn.

Application to the school was contingent on passing the New York State's Regents tests, which comprised a week of stiff academic exams. Just before those examinations began, I became sick with fu and a temperature of 104 degrees. I could barely get out of bed. "Mom, I can't go. I'm just too sick," I moaned.

"Unless you're dead, you're going!" she said. Nothing was keeping me from taking those tests for a possible scholarship.

Mom pumped me with aspirin. She gave me so much juice I felt as though I was floating. During lunchtime she was there. "How are you feeling?" she asked.

"Not so good."

She had another quart and a half of orange juice. "Drink it," she ordered. I drank most of it at her urging. She was my coach cheering me on to battle. At the end of the day, Mom took me home, rubbed me with rubbing alcohol and put me to bed. For the next day's test I thought I knew what my dad must have felt when he was a boxer. There were more workups. With my mom's encouragement, therapy, and attention, I finished the tests.

After about a month's wait, the results were in and the acceptance letter was given to Sister Charles. She opened the letter and we all saw her expression evidencing total disbelief. I had won the scholarship! Of course, she congratulated me.

Mother Superior laughed at the other nuns and told them, "I told all of you that he would do it." And so did my mother. Getting that scholarship was difficult, but it was just another beginning.

Eighth grade graduation came with the announcement of awards for excellence in various subjects. Except for the religion medal, which went to Barbara Michele, I won all the awards. It was then that Barbara took notice of me! "Francis, can you come to my graduation party?" she asked. What a finish! I felt like Seabiscuit coming out of nowhere and winning the race.

Chapter 10

Bishop Loughlin High School

High school was unbelievably tough. My days at Bishop Loughlin remind me of what Marine training must be like. The LaSale brothers, who also ran Manhattan College, gave homework that often kept me up until eleven o'clock at night or later.

Physical exercise was an integral part of the program, and Bishop Loughlin's sports program was one of the best in New York City. Its track team was tops. Everyone, and I mean everyone, was required to be on the track team. We ran, ran, and ran some more, and then we won, won, and won some more.

The LaSale brothers practiced tough love with an emphasis on tough. But it worked. Because of this demand for athletics, I was trained in track and field, and learned to play tennis.

In track, the coach had me run distance. That was not my strength. I was born with a sinus condition that slowed me down although I did well at short distances. Despite that physical hindrance, the coach forced me into long-distance running. And, this arduous requirement certainly developed my determination.

The school was a long way from our little farm in Dix Hills, Long Island. I wanted to go to Bishop Loughlin, but also break out of Brooklyn and be a farmer. My parents had agreed to let me live at the farm and commute. "You have to pay for your transportation if you want to stay there," my dad said. I knew my farm stand could bring in the needed money.

Long Island Railroad at Deer Park was a mile and a half walking distance. I'd get in the first car next to the steam loco motor, open the window and breathe in the early morning air, even with the smoke from the steam engine. I was a country boy.

The train left the station about six a. m. My mother would cook and pack meals for me so all I had to do was heat them. Some of my farm jobs were to feed the chickens and milk the goats morning and evening. It proved to be a long day, but I was determined that I was not going to be locked into living in Brooklyn.

There was little time for after-school activities with the travel involved. But at age seventeen, I decided to try out for the baseball team. I don't know why; I knew I couldn't be on the team. There was something within me wanting to find out if I could make it, and proving that I could.

At tryouts, I was called to bat. On the first pitch, knocked the ball out of the park, and the next three hits were also out of the park.

The coach was obviously satisfied. "There's a position on the team for you," he said.

"I can't make the practices, or games. It's too far," I explained.

"Well, that's too bad, Francis. You would've been good with the team."

After graduating from Bishop Loughlin, I was exhausted from the intellectual and physical challenges. Jim Duffy was a close friend in high school. We both applied to Iona College, a Catholic institution (what else?) that was overseen by the Irish Christian brothers and boy, were they Irish!

Back then colleges had two graduations each year, January and June Jim and I were both accepted, and in January 1954 we started classes. Today most graduations are held in the spring, I think that is a mistake. By having two graduations, the employment market was spread out over the year rather than fling graduates onto the market all at once. This is something for our society to rethink.

Initially at Iona, I signed up to major in history, a subject I really enjoyed. I soon discovered that Bishop Loughlin not only prepared students for college, but also actually taught on a college level. I found the courses easy except for philosophy, which was new and challenging. The history classes were not introducing me to anything new and challenging, and so I changed my major to economics. It was a difficult subject, but proved necessary.

There were many other obstacles, and also delightful times at Iona, but I had no idea how much they would affect my overall life's education.

Chapter 11

College, Politics, and Goats

After high school graduation, I entered Iona College, in New Rochelle New York. It was founded in 1940 by the Congregation of Christian Brothers, which originated in Ireland.

The Korean War had ended about six months before, and under the GI Bill, a government program paid for war veterans to attend college or vocational school. Thus, our class was comprised of mostly Korean War veterans who took advantage of this great benefit.

Almost all the freshmen were veterans and much older than I was. That was a substantial advantage for me, as veterans brought their experiences, especially those of the war, to the educational table. These veterans would bring their varied and insightful impressions to our assigned book and research readings. The contributions of these life-experienced individuals to subjects were stimulating, and I learned many valuable lessons from them.

My good friend James Duffy and I were freshmen together. We both had parents who were immigrants, his from Ireland, and mine from Italy, and our being first-generation Americans added to the experience and education mix of our class.

Originally, my declared major was to be history because I love the subject. After a short time, I realized that I had already developed a natural aptitude for it and changed my major to economics. This proved to be a challenging field and would play a most important part in my business and professional life. I was fortunate to have some fine professors, and being a young entrepreneur and running my farm store, I certainly placed well in class.

James and I were both conservatives of Republican persuasion and the student body was mostly Democrats. The school had a political organization called the Social Science Federation, which had a mere ten members. James and I would turn that club around.

I was elected president of the society and within one year, we had more than one hundred active, passionate, and conservative members. Being an active person, I was elected as president to two other clubs, as well as vice-president of another where I talked to members about The Social Science Federation. The changeover in the overall campus political philosophy was due to several circumstances.

First: It was the first time in twenty years that a Republican president was in office. Dwight D. Eisenhower was inaugurated in January 1953. For the first time in years, Republicans controlled congress for the first two of Eisenhower's eight years in office.

Second: Iona College was predominantly populated by Irish- Americans and Italian-Americans. Italians were generally inclined toward being self-employed and establishing their own businesses. The Irish, on the other hand, were mostly directed towards government service. Subsequently, our conservative Italian students were able to convince a good number of those from Irish families to join a Republican approach.

Third: Also around this time, we had a Republican and Irish-American, Senator Joseph McCarthy, heading the Senate Permanent Subcommittee on Investigations, which scrutinized the existence of communists and Soviet spies in government. From April twenty-second to June seventeenth of 1954, the hearings of this committee were televised. There were vehement pros and cons to Joe McCarthy.

Fourth: *God and Man at Yale*, a book by William Buckley, was the talk of students during my tenure as president of the Social Science Federation. Based on Buckley's undergraduate experiences at Yale University, he claimed that faculty pressured students into believing a liberal ideology and tried to weaken their religious beliefs. The Social Science Federation had a very vibrant and vocal membership, and invited Whitaker Chambers (a former member of the Communist Party in the United States) and Alger Hiss (a Harvard Law School graduate accused of being a Soviet spy) to the school to debate the fiery issue of the day: whether there were communists in government.

We almost pulled this off, but at the last minute this debate was canceled. We learned it was due to the interference of the archbishop of New York, Cardinal Francis Spellman, who was associated with influential political persons, and a close associate of President Franklin D. Roosevelt.

I learned of this after being called to the college president's office. Brother William Barnes sat me down and offered me a cigar, which I politely refused.

"Cardinal Spellman's office is very annoyed with your Social Science Federation," he began.

"Why is that?" I asked.

"You are making a lot of noise for Republicans, especially with the Joe McCarthy supporters. Cardinal Spellman receives a lot of financial support from Democrats who are also upset with you," he said. "Cardinal Spellman wants the club disbanded and all the officers to resign."

I felt myself getting upset, breathing faster, and clenching my teeth. "Iona teaches us about our first amendment rights of free speech."

"The first amendment has strict restrictions on this campus. As the president of Iona, I could terminate your stay at the college," he stated with a long stare.

Many of my friends in the club gathered at my parents' house and we explored ways to fight this unjust act. My father spoke to us as men. "We must remind ourselves of the famous Pickett's Charge at Gettysburg and the slaughter that occurred due to stubbornness and foolhardiness," he said in reference to Major General George Pickett's failed assault on the Union infantry in Gettysburg.

"Brother Barnes holds the high ground. He could destroy your future careers with expulsion," he said. "This predicament will pass." We listened to my father, and even in our indignation and outrage, we knew he was right and reluctantly agreed to take his advice. I waited until the last minute to submit my resignation as president of the Social Science Federation.

A year later, as my father predicted, the Joe McCarthy hearings were a song of the past. Brother Barnes called me into his office and asked me to reorganize the Social Science Federation. I did and it was again a great success.

College continued to drain my finances. To increase my cash flow, I purchased a large Ford station wagon and recruited paying passengers for the drive to and from school. In addition, I worked out an agreement with Iona College to supply the religious faculty and training center for the brothers with bags of fresh potatoes from my neighbor's farm in Dix Hills, Long Island.

Iona was well supplied with my potatoes, and I continued bringing them to the kitchen until one day the Chinese cook came after me with his cleaver raised high saying in his inimitable dialect, "Potatoes here, potatoes there, potatoes everywhere! No more potatoes!"

Despite his broken English, his cleaver and body language clearly conveyed his message! I stopped bringing potatoes for a few months, and later at lesser quantities, but continued to make money.

The French Club also wanted to raise money by having a dance, and the committee asked me to suggest someone for an inexpensive guest appearance. After a while, I smiled, and said, "I think Napoleon and his wife, Josephine, would be appropriate. We'll promote the dance by saying: *Two famous guests will be at the dance and their identities will not be disclosed until then*."

No one knew who would be coming as Napoleon and Josephine. The club rented a large van in which I could bring the unidentified guests. I drove all the way out to Long Island and went to my Italian goat-raising friends and asked them to lend me a horned buck and a small doe: Napoleon and Josephine.

When I arrived at the college the French Club had a sold-out attendance. With excitement running rampant as to who the guests were, I dropped the ramps of the van and led Napoleon and Josephine onto the dance floor. Two of my buddies followed the goats and were equipped with shovels to collect any discharged pellets.

I walked the goats all around introducing Napoleon and Josephine to a hysterically laughing crowd, especially when my buddies would miss the goats' pellets falling on the floor.

After the dance, I loaded the goats for their return home, and nor far from my destination, I was stopped by a New York State trooper. "What are you hauling? And where are you going?" he asked.

"I'm returning celebrity guests from our college dance to their home," I responded.

After peering in the van, he said, "Goats at three a.m. You have got to be crazy."

I explained what happened in greater detail, and the officer let me go. I suspect he thought I was not quite three, but only two sheets to the wind, although the non-alcoholic version.

On many occasions, I represented our organization and the college at other learning institutions, and of course, posited the conservative position. These trips and speeches proved most enjoyable and challenging and caused me to develop a very acceptable and easy approach to public speaking. I never feared speaking to a crowd, thanks to the support and example of my mother. She loved talking to people and she encouraged me to do the same.

I remember vividly one particular "encouragement" came one day when my mom took me to a movie, and a show. Back in the early forties, movie theaters would present two film features and also live performances. This particular day, an acrobat asked for a volunteer for his act. Without hesitation, my mother picked me up and put me on the stage. I was young, maybe six or seven, and the performer took my hand and I stood there, and looked out onto the audience. The acrobat took me by my hands and swung me around and around as he skated on the stage. When he was through, the thrilled audience clapped loudly and I liked the applause! Since that experience, I've had no fears of public speaking.

Since my college years, I have given speeches and addresses on such topics as sheep and wool production, entrepreneurial skills, economics, constitutional and criminal law and ethics, at places such as the University of Virginia' Entrepreneurial Club, Cornell University, Hampton College, Michigan State University, and various groups and organizations.

Even today, at my parish in Staunton, Virginia, I serve as a commentator, lecturer and Extraordinary Eucharistic Minister (one who is not ordained but may distribute Holy Communion). I still like it!

Before college graduation my father strongly suggested that I take up a major profession. I wanted to please him and applied to only one law school, St. John's University in New York City. Unbeknownst to me, the faculty, upon hearing I applied to law school, sent many letters on my behalf to the admissions department at St. John's. I was admitted without ever taking its law-qualification test.

Six months into law school it was discovered that I was admitted without the test and was asked to complete it for their record. I never heard how I did. What mattered was that I was at St. John's Law School, which opened up many more experiences and stories to tell.

Chapter 12

Mail Call

In 1956 some of my buddies at college asked me to join them working as Christmas temps for the US Post Office. I agreed only to get the experience of working for someone other than myself. This would be the one and only time I worked for another company aside from adjunct teaching assignments.

Since I was living in rural Long Island, I was assigned to the Pennsylvania Street Post Office in midtown Manhattan. The first day's assignment had me sorting general mail along with others in a large sorting area. Soon after commencing work, I was told by the supervisor to "slow down." This remark would be repeated throughout my employment with the post office.

The next day I was moved to the pigeonhole boxes sorting individual mail. That department's supervisor came up to me and said, "You see that guy in the next station sorting the mail? Well, he can't read or write. He was sent here by the politicians."

"What are you going to do?" I asked.

"I'll just get someone else to resort it."

On the third day I was part of a crew delivering packages, and later that week, was sent solo to deliver mail to an apartment complex in a residential area. Given a large bag of mail, a key, and no instructions, I was sent to an unfamiliar route.

After finding the starting point, I proceeded to drop the letters at their appropriate addresses, but could not figure out the purpose of the key. I asked someone who apparently lived in the complex, and found that he did not speak English.

Showing him the key I managed to get across my question. He took the key from the long chain attached to the mailbag, placed it in the master box lock of the apartment's mailbox cover and opened it to expose a large number of individual slots. I got it. I put the mail in accordingly and am still thankful to that individual. I proceeded down the streets and finished all my deliveries and returned to the post office station.

The postmaster met me. "Are you finished delivering all that mail?"

"Yes sir." It had taken me an hour and a half.

He gave me another bag filled with mail to be delivered, "Go and get lost until five o'clock."

"I know now how the system works. I can move the mail along faster."

"Just get lost until five."

I was able to finish that sack in forty-five minutes. I enjoy working. Idle time and I are not compatible. I didn't understand how "getting lost" was part of my responsibility in working for the post office.

The next day I returned to the Pennsylvania Avenue Post Office with four other employees to unload trucks laden with boxes of packages. A conveyor ran about fifteen feet from the trailer to the dock of the post office building. Four people were assigned to unload one box moving on the elevator at the slowest speed possible. I was quickly tired of this and went inside the trailer and began carrying several boxes at a time.

"Hey, slow down," said the supervisor.

"This is my normal speed" were just wasted words.

The next week I was sent to the sub-basement where I was to lay out the empty sacks onto a pushcart and line up the carts next to the empty bag warehouse. I did this for several hours and noticed that the train of carts was hardly moving, I walked to the starting point and to my dismay the two who were there to unload were fast asleep on the mountain of empty sacks.

I walked upstairs and told the supervisor about this hold up. He handed me a tennis ball and said, "Go play ball with yourself."

So I did. At five o'clock, after not seeing the carts moving, I went to the supervisor again. "I won't be returning to 'work' tomorrow. I'm going back to school."

This was an unbelievable experience for me. I want to believe that the present postal system isn't like that.

Chapter 13

Dancing With the Holy Ghost

When I was a young altar boy, I thought seriously of becoming a priest. What a wonderful life, I thought it would be to say mass, preach, hear confessions, and administer the other sacraments. It seemed that it would be an ideal life to combine with farming.

As I grew up and was in high school, I realized that there was more to being a priest. Such as taking orders from bishops who are saintly, and from some who are political animals and speaking political correctness. The former would be great, but not the latter.

I would never disagree with my church on issues of faith and morals, but some bishops are bound to the mode of political correctness, which is not for me. Therefore, I chose the path of staying active in the Catholic Church by holding down volunteer ministerial duties such as Extraordinary Eucharistic Minister, Liturgical Minister, and Commentator at mass. I am also a member (fourth degree) of the Knights of Columbus, a founder, and a former Charter Grand Knight of Counsel 670 in my parish.

Being known as a good sympathetic listener, I have also been known to give effective advice. Many attorneys who hold a doctorate in law, such as I do, are doctors of law (juris doctoris). So in the same way a medical doctor uses medication for healing, I issue prescriptions for living a prudent life. Sometimes as with medical prescriptions, clients/patients don't take the advice, and rip up the prescriptions to their detriment.

When I was seventeen, I ventured out on my first date with a lovely girl whose father was a doctor in Bensonhurst, Brooklyn. I was a total flop because I did not know how to act properly on a date. I hesitate to put my arm around the girl during the movies or to hold her hand. I was surely insecure in my actions and it apparently showed. She didn't agree to a follow-up date.

On my next date I knew better. I maintained a more relaxed posture with another lovely girl.

On one date, she stunned me with an announcement. "I'm going to become a Maryknoll nun," she said.

Like me, she was a beginner at dating so we learned from each other. For a while I was sure I must have given her the wrong impression of dating, driving her to become a nun! She wrote to me many times after indicating her love for the church and prayed for me. I was actually happy to have a nun's prayers for my further adventures with girls.

What a change there has been from dating in the 1940's and 50s compared to today's casual boy-girl relations. Every girl I dated, and there were many, were Catholic girls except for two - a fine Jewish teacher, and a Protestant who eventually became my wife.

Mondays in high school were full of conversation among the guys about the dates they had over the weekend. They usually went something like this:

"Joe, how did you make out with Mary?"

"Not so good, she's a Catholic. But I did get a kiss."

If a guy got to pet his girl a little, that was big news, and also grounds for confession on Saturday afternoon.

Bishop Loughlin High School was for boys. There was a Catholic girls' school across the street where the girls were taught by nuns. On Friday afternoons, our school invited the girls for dancing and the good nuns would chaperone.

When a guy got real close to a girl while dancing, a nun would approach, slide her hand between the couple and say, "Make room for the Holy Ghost!"

The poor nuns seemed to be always busy making room for the Holy Ghost. I assure you with them around, and they always seemed to be around (thank goodness), there weren't many out-of-wedlock pregnancies.

While attending Iona College, the men would go over to the College of New Rochelle. Which was also run by good nuns. There he encountered fewer intrusions by the nuns. I think the nuns felt that by this lime, marriage was in order and many marriages did ensue.

Iona's demographics included forty-eight percent Italian, forty-eight percent Irish, and four percent others. Parents of the Irish and Italians did not want their children marrying outside of their nationality.

For instance, I was very active in college, holding down three presidencies and one vice presidency. I was also chief cheerleader. As a cheerleader, I took a lovely redhead, Irish as they come, with her folks straight from the old sod, to a basketball game where I was cheering.

After a couple of dates, I was at her house to pick her up for another game. Her parents asked me into the living room.

"What are your intentions with our daughter?" asked her father.

"No intentions intended." I said.

"That's good, because we would never allow our daughter to marry an Italian boy."

That attitude sprung from both sides of the nationality fence. There was no question that these two groups were quite different. The Irish were restrained emotionally and beer drinkers, and Italians were known to be unrestrained emotionally and controlled wine drinkers. But......both had a common interest in the Catholic Church and that is why they did intermarry. Back then, Vince Lombardi, an Italian and his Irish wife, Mary, had a great marriage.

Of three hundred or more graduates from Iona College, I know of only one divorce, although there may have been others of which I am not aware. In the 1940's and 1950's the divorce rate was about five percent compared to today's fifty.

Back then...

On Saturday nights, I would often go to a Catholic parish dance at St. Joseph's in Astoria, Long Island. The priests were in attendance, alcohol beverages were not allowed, but we had a great time dancing. "Fooling around" was not permitted.

"Your bodies house the Holy Ghost and you are not to defile yours or another's body," we were constantly told. Respect for each other was the rule. Men's and boys' hats came off when a woman entered the elevator and they would open car doors for the ladies. Women and girls wore modest clothing so the guys would not get emotionally charged up.

When a guy started to act up "too much" a girl would say "no!" and no was the rule. Back then, girls were counseled that there would be no bed (no sexual intercourse) until marriage, and a boy had to have five-thousand dollars in his bank account for security. Respect, for both, was the key.

There was another saying and oh so valid: *Why buy the cow when you can get all the milk you want at no cost?* In other words, today, most girls make themselves sexually available and so the guys usually don't bother marrying them. Girls seem to give guys all the advantages without the responsibilities. I have heard this statement more times than you can ever imagine. "I don't trust him/her. I played around with her/him before marriage and what's to now stop her/him from playing around with others?" Trust. In most cases like those, it's just not there.

Back then, you trusted your spouse. Diane, and I did not go to bed with each other before marriage and we trust each other implicitly to this very day after forty-four years of marriage.

One of my teachers told our class that women control the morals of society. When most women demand high morals, as they did back in the 1940s and 1950s, men respected those morals. Today, most women demand nothing in morality and men are so eager to comply.

Religious sacrifices seem, to me, to have gone by the wayside. A factor in vogue for Catholics before Vatican II in the 1960s was not to eat or drink (except water) after midnight if they were planning to receive Holy Communion the following day. Catholics were not permitted to eat meat on Fridays. We were told to fast on Fridays during Lent and to give up good things as a sacrifice as a way to build up a resistance to temptations. It helped. Most of those things today are now optional, but encouraged.

During those dances I attended and loved so long ago, girls would line up on one side of the dance floor and the fellows on the opposite side. The fellows would be the ones to ask a girl to dance with them. Often there were a few girls who weren't asked. It made me uncomfortable for them. They came with great anticipation to have fun dancing and they could leave, not having danced. I would routinely dance with them and it would just bring a smile on their faces and a sparkle in their eyes. I loved seeing that.

Some guys would say, "Why do you want to dance with the dogs?"

"I hate that expression, and lay off. There are no such things as human dogs."

The saying sticks and stones may break my bones, but words will never hurt me is so untrue! Words have lasting effects and can cause more harm than sticks and stones. I learned early in life that words can be devastating or can be uplifting.

Sometimes when I see a person looking obviously downtrodden especially in church, I go to them and give them an uplifting statement like, "Even though it's raining today, sun is still shining and tomorrow we will see the sun again." I am always uplifted by the fact that I have, along with a multitude of others, read the final chapter of the Bible where it says "we win the devil loses," so why not be upbeat.

What moved me to have empathy for people with disadvantages? My father did. Although he stood only five feet tall, he was built like an ox, but oh, what a gentle a man he was. He routinely ignored disparaging remarks from others, as I cried inside for him. Some people would make fun of him for his limited height.

Because of him, I swore I would never use words to hurt a person with disadvantages and would do whatever I could to help others.

And so came many instances for me to practice that oath to myself.

Chapter 14

Wearing More Than One Hat

My direct marketing was a success from the beginning, and led my thoughts toward a future career centered on that narrow career objective. My parents, especially my father, had some other ideas for me. Three months before graduating from college, the three of us discussed my future career plans.

"What do you want to do after college?" asked my mom.

"I plan to continue with my winning farm business."

My dad said he thought that with my education thus far, it would be foolish to stop there since it was obvious that I enjoyed school, which was true.

"Farming is not a foolproof approach to making a living," he added. "What if there is a drought? What if your retail location suddenly changed due to road redirection, population changes, or something else?"

Dad knew I enjoyed my business so he put it in a very convincing approach. "Keep going with your business but have a backup in case things go bad, have a profession."

With careful consideration, I thought about the many times he gave me advice and I failed to listen, much to my chagrin. There were times that I listened and was in a winning position due to taking his advice. I came to the conclusion that I had an extremely wise father. In my mind he was a giant and my greatest hero.

As a young man, weighing only one-hundred-forty pounds, he picked up the front end of a Model T Ford in a friendly contest of strength. Dad was a winning boxer representing his local Knights of Columbus council at the highly contested Catholic Youth Organization (also known as CYO) programs. This was my father. A giant in my eye and yet a very soft-spoken man who chose his words carefully. I decided to proceed with his advice. Before going the lawyer route I considered alternative professions and decided lawyering would be the best and would work with the farm business.

I decided that just maybe being an attorney could be of value to both the community and to my family and that proved to be so. It is amazing how much good can be accomplished by a really good attorney.

After graduation, I prepared for the New York Bar examination, and took it at New York City Center in midtown Manhattan. There were a large number of applicants taking the test. I considered these two days living hell. The pressure of both time and content was insane. They say that the New York bar is the toughest in the country. Two people had mental breakdowns. That first day, one started a fire at his desk. Both were carried out and sent to hospitals.

Eventually I passed the bar and was sworn in. That afternoon I received a telephone call from my first client. It proved to be a very complicated divorce case and helped me to learn quickly the differences between the theories of law as opposed to its practical application.

I should mention that a year before I had set up my insurance agency and also income tax preparation operations. Dad gave me space in his garden center to get started. I was amazed that my law practice grew so quickly. I never worked for a law firm. They call it "the practice of law" and I did a lot of practicing and continue to do so to this day.

There were several advantages. First was my farm stand. The public knew that I was attending law school and when I was admitted to the bar, they figured I didn't cheat them by selling tomatoes and such, so they concluded that I would be honest as a lawyer.

I asked many questions starting out and especially of the court clerks. They were so helpful and guided me to the necessary case files to put me on the right track. I was forced to learn quickly.

On the opposite side of Dad's property in Roslyn Heights, next to his nursery and garden center lived Mr. and Mrs. Pearsall. They were a wonderful couple who had gorgeous grounds surrounding their lovely home and garage.. I loved to listen to their stories, about their early lives, and experiences of being black in the north. Mrs. Pearsall would routinely bring over homemade blueberry muffins for me.

The Pearsall's were in their late eighties or early nineties when, started my practice and suggested that I buy their property where I could set up my law office.

"I can't afford your property," I admitted.

Mrs. Pearsall looked at me. "Do you have any money for a down payment?"

"Well, I've saved five thousand dollars," I said.

The Pearsall's sold me their property for thirty-five thousand dollars and even took back a mortgage. I will always be so grateful to them. My dad, and Uncle Val helped me make a beautiful office out of their home and I continued my law career in that beautiful setting next to my dad's garden center and farm stand.

Just as in farming, I wanted to be on my own, and never worked for a law firm. My father knew that I wanted to support myself, on my own. It was truly worth the effort to go to law school and as my father said, it would prove to be a financial stabilizer in my life.

My first law secretary was Aggie Massaro. She had been a legal secretary some years before at one of the most prestigious law firms in Manhattan and shared with me her large legal form portfolio. What a resource! She was so helpful and I am so thankful for her assistance, especially in my early career days.

I had another secretary for the insurance and tax preparation work by the name of Roslyn Frieland, a Jewish woman with a great personality. I learned much about the Jewish faith from her and became good friends with her and her husband.

I attended their son's bar mitzvah at their synagogue and was so impressed with the religious terror that I witnessed that day. How anyone, especially Christians, could have anything but admiration for the Jews is beyond me. Our Christian faith's foundation is based on what we call the Old Testament and the Jews call it the Torah.

Roslyn had a problem however, and it caused me to have great empathy for her people because of the Holocaust of World War II. She lost her grandparents and cousins to the Nazis and had great bitterness to anything

German. Six million Jews and three million Christians lost their lives to that horror. We had many discussions about her family's loss. She told me about the several boatloads of Jews that were expelled by Hitler. When the boats approached the United States, they were refused entry into the US by President Franklin D. Roosevelt. The boats returned to Germany because no country would take them, and were never to be seen again. What horrible loss of lives of such wonderful people.

I have known many Jews and hold them in high esteem. I recall bumper stickers reading *My God Was a Jewish Carpenter*. Enough said about that.

Chapter 15
Bucking the Current at Law School

St. John's School of Law in Brooklyn was the only law school I applied to and told my father that if I were not accepted there, I would not go any further with the lawyer idea. To my chagrin I was accepted.

My first day at St. John's, located in downtown Brooklyn, proved to be most discouraging and disturbing. I felt like a fish out of water. Three hundred new students were assembled in an auditorium.

The assistant dean, Dr. Harold McNeice, addressed those assembled with this remark: Gentlemen, ladies, (there were sixteen women out of three hundred) look to your right and look to your left. I will graduate from this class a total of one hundred. That means two out of three will eventually be dismissed from St. John's. It is in your hands who will stay and who will go. Starting now, the elimination process begins.

What a way to open a new part of my life.

The demographics also concerned me. Students were from the big city whose fathers were lawyers or judges and it felt strange to me. I was the only one with a farm background, and proud of it. Although on my mother's side, I had three second cousins in the legal profession, two of whom were lawyers. One was Carl Soviero, a United States diplomat in Naples, Italy. The other, Joseph Soviero, would become a member of the New York State Assembly and eventually a Supreme Court judge in Brooklyn, the highest trial court in the New York court system. The third family member was Edmund Palmer, a judge in the first federal circuit in Manhattan. Despite that, I still considered myself a lone country boy amongst professional wannabes.

There were some students who had no family members connected to the legal profession. One of them was a black veteran of the Korean War, Charles Rangel, from Harlem. Although Charlie and I differed politically a hundred and eighty degrees apart, we respected each other and became and still are friends. Today he is a senior member representing New York in the House of Representatives.

At the time my father still owned his small farm in Dix Hills, Long Island. I lived there, and ran a vegetable and fruit stand in Roslyn Heights while commuting to school in downtown Brooklyn. (Years later the law school relocated to a beautiful campus at Hillcrest, Queens County, Long Island.)

At the close of that first day at St. John's, I returned to my farm stand to speak with my mother who agreed to attend to my farm stand while I was in school. She was sitting in a rocking chair as I proceeded to toss my law books into a nearby empty chair and announced, "I'm not going back to law school."

My wise mother continued to rock herself and stated, "You are the first of your dad's family to graduate from college. You don't need to continue, I'll tell the family that you quit."

I took strong resentment to this and said, "I am not quitting."

Mom replied, "It sure looks like it to me; your books are over there. But it's ok. You can quit."

With this I snatched up my books. "I will go back and finish and hand you the degree."

"Do whatever," she said. And so I returned to law school.

Each day before leaving for classes I would set up the farm stand with fruits and vegetables so my mother could sell them. Rising before five a.m., I'd feed my goats, chickens and other members of the animal family and get dressed to walk about a mile to the Long Island train station. I always sat in the car nearest the coal-fired locomotive and swayed the train ride. To this day, I don't know how I managed this balancing act, but I did. Each year, the farm stand stayed open for the summer and ended November first.

Law school was the toughest educational experience of my life. My days started with three hundred students and eventually, as predicted by the dean, two hundred would fail. I promised my mother that I would continue and so I reluctantly carried on.

At first, adapting was an emotional challenge. I didn't appreciate having to spend so much time reading case after case all day. Subconsciously, I tried to be a farmer in a very strict law environment.

One day I was riding an elevator to class when the assistant dean of the school stepped on.

"I see you don't have on a tie or jacket," he said.

"I don't like jackets," I replied.

"Where is your tie?"

"I don't like them either," I said.

"Where are your books?" he persisted.

"They are at my farm, but I do my homework, Sir. I just don't haul my books around."

"That's very un-lawyer like. I don't think you'll succeed here. I'll see that you don't." he said.

"Well, Sir, I don't think that will happen. I've promised my mother that I'd finish. You don't know my mother. She wants this degree for me and I intend to get it in spite of what you think."

And the war was on. As it turned out, after my cocky responses, the assistant dean got the word out to my professors who made life really tough on me. There wasn't a day or a subject that I wasn't called upon to report my case, and I was always ready. That school gave me the toughest time imaginable, but I was determined to complete the essentials for that degree.

At one point, I was required to take corporation law. It was as dull as it gets, so I memorized the statutes so I could get on and out of Dullsville. Upon completing my final examination in that subject, and after I discussed the examination with other students, our answer differed. I was confident I had the correct answers. When our papers were returned, I was relieved to see that I had all the right answers but upset that I received a B. I went marching to my professor.

"All of my answers are correct," I protested. "Why do I have a B?"

"Yes, all of your answers are right," he said glancing over my paper. "But here, see there is no comma. Over here, the spelling is incorrect. Sorry, Mr. Chester, this is not grade-A work."

"This was a three-hour exam given in two hours," I implored. "I spent the full two hours writing. That's not fair."

I had to live with the B...and the professor's smiling face as I left.

The professors may have been out to get me, but among my peers, I did not have enemies. Charlie Rangel and I both were nominated for president of the class. I withdrew my nomination in favor of Charlie with the statement that he needed it more than I, as I would be going into practice on my own and didn't feel I need the distinction on my resume.

At law school, classes ended at twelve-thirty in the afternoon followed by mass at which I served. It was expected that we would spend the afternoons studying. I would, especially in winter and spring, go across the street to the Supreme Court and listen to some of the more famous criminal cases imaginable. Lots of Mafia cases with their big-time lawyers. It was fascinating and a great learning experience.

My mother told me that we never had any family member in the Mafia and I believe that to be true because our family, along with other good Italian families, despised the Mafioso for giving our culture a bad name.

One of the rules in law school was: no jobs. A second rule: no other studies except law. Well, I violated both. Earnings from the farm stand provided money for my tuition. They also gave me the necessary stimulation and drive to be an individual practitioner.

While enrolled, law school was to be exclusive, but I reasoned if I were to have an office, I wanted to get a head start. So I enrolled in a one-year course at Pratts Institute to qualify for a broker's insurance license. Classes were held in downtown Manhattan and commuting there was an insane idea, because getting home at midnight wore me out. Surprisingly I wound up with the highest mark of the class, although my grades in law school were not ones to write home about.

All three years at St. John's drove my emotions for it from love do hate. The love came into play when I took constitutional law and criminal law. Those were exciting subjects. One of the constitutional cases that really had my attention was *Karamatsu vs. United States.*

This case involved President Franklin D. Roosevelt's 1942 proclamation that approximately one-hundred-ten-thousand Japanese nationals, and American citizens of Japanese descent be moved from the West Coast in guarded camps. I considered this case a black eye in American history. Why not Germans or Italians? A logical explanation was never presented.

The benefits of being an attorney, and understanding the role of one in society, began to make sense to me. How much value an attorney can be to a community is determined by how truthful he or she is to the principles learned in law school. I came to the conclusion that just maybe being an attorney could be worthwhile to both my community and to my family and that proved to be so. It is amazing how much good can be accomplished by an exceptional attorney.

In May of 1960 I graduated from law school. I would like to say in the top of my class, but truth be told it was not so due to my ambivalence. On the day of graduation the assistant dean and some of my professors came over and congratulated me. "You owe us a thank you," said one professor.

"Why?"

"We realized that you actually did have what it takes to make a good lawyer and the way to get you into high gear was to make life tough," he said. And that they did.

My mother and dad took turns holding my law degree all that day. It made me so happy to see my immigrant parents proud of me. Those three years were truly worth the effort and I wanted to prove that it would be everything my father said it would be - including a financial stabilizer in my life.

So, the next step was to pass the New York Bar exam.

Chapter 16

Farm Stand = Tuition

Even after starting my law practice, my small farm was a comfort and allowed me to make a good living. Over the years, I had been able to pay cash each year for college, law school, and later for graduate school. After earning a juris doctorate (law degree), I also received a BA in economics, and a MA in political science with a certificate in international law.

Aside from all of the schooling, farming was what I loved. It was at the forefront of all my educational pursuits. From the first days of my business with a little red wagon, I soon learned what customers wanted and always provided quality produce and service.

My father bought land on Powerhouse Road, a heavily traveled state highway in Roslyn Heights, Long Island and I set up a farm stand there. I discovered that when business slacked off, having someone park their vehicle by my stand increased business. Painting the stand yellow was another trick of the trade.

As the business thrived, I learned valuable lessons. Once I decided to reduce the price of my sweet corn to gain market share. I went from sixty-nine to forty-nine cents per dozen, and customers wanted to know the reason. No explanations satisfied them so after one week of this I realized that reducing prices on exceptional quality was a poor policy. I went back to the old price and was then greeted with statements like: "You got your old corn back..." and "Glad to see this corn is on the stand again," when it was actually the same product.

When a local chain store reduced its corn prices to twenty- nine cents per thirteen ears, it could not give corn away, And so that stores manager gave up selling corn for twenty-nine cents per thirteen ears versus my sixty-nine cents a dozen saying he would no longer sell sweet corn as long as I sold any corn.

There were many other lessons that taught me to be a better entrepreneur. One was not to be afraid to take reasonable chances. You may lose from time to time but when you hit a homerun, all the past misses will be forgotten.

I learned so much from that operation - marketing, display, money management, organization, production of fruit and vegetables among others. I recall sometime around 1954, Labor Day, which was always our busiest day of the season and my farmer friend and his tall Jamaican helpers picked two thousand ears of sweet corn for that day. I could usually count on my parents to help me on that holiday.

I was shocked when they told me that they were going to go out and leave the stand solely for me to run. How was I going to handle the crowds? Well, I had no choice so I made the best of it. I organized myself by preparing simple tricks. I put various sized bags around my belt. Kept the scale close by and so I proceeded with the day's customers. I learned to judge weight and math really well. I was able to take care of several customers at one time. This taught me to be able to multitask all at once.

When my folks came back that early evening, I unloaded all the money I took in. It was over five-hundred dollars. My mother, in her inimitable style said, "Your stand just shits money - it's unbelievable!" That day alone almost paid for my college tuition for the whole year, minus books and miscellaneous expenses.

Tuition then was sixteen dollars per credit with eighteen credits for one semester. Later in 1957, law school would be twenty-five dollars per credit.

A farm friend had Jamaicans to work his sweet corn fields, and I enjoyed working with them. We would start pulling corn around sunrise, load the corn on my truck, and I would take it a few miles away to my stand.

One year, I asked if I could get sweet corn as early as July Fourth to get a jump on the market. I discovered that a recent agricultural graduate from Cornell was raising sweet corn near Orient Point - the farthest eastern point on Long Island off of Peconic Bay. He would start harvesting sweet corn before the Fourth and would take the ferry across the sound and sell it in Boston. I made a deal with him and started to haul the corn to my stand. It was about a three-and-a-half hour drive round trip, but I had corn when no one else did and I reaped a healthy business, both retail and wholesale. It necessitated getting up at four a.m., returning and working the stand until six in the evening, nap and head to the Washington market two or three times a week.

In a few years, I would buy my own small Long Island farm in Mill Neck and take option on some additional land. In addition I leased some of the estates' land to graze my sheep. The funds came from my farm stand, not the law practice, which did not start until 1961.

Chapter 17

Lessons Learned

My first personal injury case was a real learning experience in the practice of law. A carpenter came to me after being injured through no fault of his own. It was around 1962 or thereabouts. I advised him that if he continued to have pain, he was to go to the doctor as needed. It was necessary to document his pain and suffering. He told me he had to work, and had no time for doctors.

Well, when I presented my demand for compensation, the medical bills came to one-hundred-sixty-five dollars, but the few medical bills did not reflect his true injuries because he worked, regardless of his pain.

The claims' officer rejected the amount of my demand saying the medical bills didn't support the demand. I retorted, "My client is an honest man and had to work."

"Buddy, you obviously are a newly minted lawyer. We don't pay for honesty; we pay based on proper medical bills and reports." The case was settled.

I hired a young man named Alex Miller as an investigator for my office whose father was an Austrian professor of law and a Jew. His father and mother escaped from Austria and managed to settle in America. Alex was their only child and born in the US and he was unbelievable as an investigator.

I won many a case because of the evidence Alex was able to uncover. One day I received a call from the Nassau County police chief who told me that Alex was embarrassing his department. In his spare time, Alex would be at the crime scene before the police and have the suspects in hand before the police arrived. I was able to get Alex to moderate his enthusiasm for investigations. He later asked me to be his godfather when he converted to the Catholic faith.

I also hired a young man as a paralegal who was also studying to be a lawyer. Richard Gumo became a fine lawyer and later joined the district attorney's office in Nassau County. By then I had five employees in my office while my farm stand (conveniently located next door) continued to operate and was as busy as ever. I would go over there from time to time to help out my mom, who was my "top" and only farm stand employee.

About that time, I received an ominous letter from the Nassau County Bar advising me that I was in ethical violation because I was advertising. Back then, marketing by attorneys was severely limited. No longer is that so. The basis of the complaint was that I was using the farm stand to generate law clients. Well, being out of law school for a short time, I was concerned. I went to my professors and asked for their advice. The answer I got was that the other lawyers were jealous and that I should fight the charge.

My dad contacted a lawyer friend of his who was also past president of the bar association. He agreed to help me, and suggested that I take my camera and go around the county taking pictures of other law offices.

"Why?" I asked.

"It will become evident." And so I gathered more than sixty pictures of attorney's offices.

One set showed sequential signs reading: Big Chief Lewis, 3 Miles Ahead; Big Chief Lewis, 1 Mile Ahead. And finally: Big Chief Lewis' Law Office, Insurance Agency and Tax Preparation. I had other photos depicting similar signs.

The night of my hearing, my attorney walked in with me, and the hearing board was surprised when they recognized him. He spread out the pictures before the board, shocking them all, and resulting with the ethics complaint dismissed. I thanked the attorney and asked him what his fee was.

"Nothing," he said. "Your father and family are the most honest and fine people I have ever known. There is no charge."

There were other times I had no defend myself. Soon after starting my practice, I was accepted into St. John's University's Graduate School for political science. After the hated years of law school I actually longed to return to the academic setting. I missed the mental gymnastics an challenges of it all.

I had purchased a beautiful red Thunderbird and I would commute from my office in Roslyn Heights to the Hillcrest campus in Queen County. I was a hotshot, young, single attorney and had rewarded myself with a new car.

Traffic was not proceeding as usual because of some construction on Northern State Parkway when I was pulled over by two New York City police officers. They looked over my car, and asked how I came about buying it. They suggested that I become a "contributor" to their personal cause. I told them I would not give a bribe. They laughed and gave me a ticket for speeding.

I was stopped three more times by these fellows and was given three additional tickets about the same time each day. They said, "You don't get the point."

I said, "I get the point all right."

I took my tickets to court and after I fought the first one, I was found not guilty. Second one, in front of the same judge, not guilty. The judge then asked me if I had more. I told her, "Yes, two more."

She asked me to bring them to her and after looking at the tickets turned to the officers and said out loud, without further evidence, "Not guilty, and not guilty."

The officers left with smiles. The judge was great, and quite perceptive I would say. I want to add that I truly respect police officers and sheriff's officers. They do an outstanding job. I believe these officers were just having a good time of it, but it did cost me valuable time to participate in their game.

Another incident took place on this same highway. One bright summer's day, I was happily driving along in the passing lane and open convertible with two young, well-endowed women was directly in front of me. They were going about twenty-five in a fifty-five mile zone, and behind me was a line of cars. I honked my horn a couple of times to no avail except for one of the women extending a finger in the air in my direction.

After honking my horn a third time, one of the full-figured women turned around in her seat, got on her knees, spewed one big spit towards me. It flew directly back in her face which she tried to remove without satisfaction. They moved over to the right and the line of traffic moved on. Justice! Right on!

I have been blessed to have had my eyes opened to justice on numerous occasions and to have played roles that resulted in it being achieved. Being an attorney is not easy, especially if you aim at righteousness. There are many temptations, but as Shakespeare eloquently said, "To thine own self be true."

When I take on a case, I try to address the cause of my client's getting into the trouble that he or she was being charged. If it's substance abuse I try to get help, psychiatric if needed. I only take substance abuse cases such as drugs or alcohol if the client will make a commitment to cooperate in all ways to change his or her life.

One day a beautiful young lady come to my office and asked me to defend her boyfriend who was charged with multiple counts of selling drugs. I told her of my conditions of representing people faced with drug charges.

The young woman across my desk said her boyfriend is not going to promise to cooperate; he just wants a good lawyer and a good defense. I refused to represent him. She pulled out a very large stack of cash. "There's ten thousand dollars here," she said. "There's more where that came from."

What a temptation! I turned her down again and told her if he decided to comply with my conditions she could come back. She couldn't believe my reaction. About a month later, I learned that she was also arrested and both she and her boyfriend eventually were sentenced to long prison terms.

There have been so many opportunities to meet wonderful people. Early in my career, I was hired by a client who was a sensitive and gentle sculptor requesting a will and some other legal work. He was also an atheist and we had some remarkable discussions on religion. Sometime after the legal work was completed, he dropped by my office and presented to me a set of leaded praying hands mounted on carefully carved wood.

"I want you to have this that I made for you because I know you will appreciate what it represents," he said. I cherish them to this day. I believe he was a Jewish man who had temporarily lost his faith because of what happened during World War II. The events of World War II were still very much alive in all of our minds in the early 1960s.

So began my life in what they call the "practice of law." I did a lot of practicing at the beginning and many more were to come.

Chapter 18

A Shepherd Meets His Mate

It was May 1966. It seemed as if I had everything a thirty-year-old man could want as far as a satisfying career in both farming and law. I was blessed with degrees from an excellent college and university, owned a fine law office building, had a flourishing law practice, an insurance agency, and a profitable direct-marketing farm operation. I also had a beautiful new home on a lovely small farm on Long Island along the North Shore where there were a large number of Thoroughbred horse farms. What else could I ask for?

Well, I wished for a wife, and envisioned one who appreciated my love of actively living the life of a sheep farmer. It was something I longed for.

It had been five years since I began practicing law. I had my small farm in Mill Neck, New York, where I was next to Oyster Bay, former home of my hero, Teddy Roosevelt. And, I had just bought a horse. Jean Sue was a registered quarter horse out of the King Ranch line and was an extremely rambunctious, but beautiful looking animal.

One Saturday morning, I was taking my mother shopping, and told Ray, who was working on the farm, to be sure to keep the gates closed. "Jean Sue seems to have wanderlust," I laughed.

But when I returned, the horse had run off. Jean Sue was gone. After scouring the adjacent woods and looking all over, I failed in my attempt to locate my energetic Jean Sue.

My father suggested calling the local village police stations to ask if there had been any reports on the whereabouts of Jean Sue. After several calls, an officer at the police station in Upper Brookville, New York, advised me that he had received a phone call from a young girl who had found a horse. He gave me her phone number and I called it.

After I identified myself to the young woman, she was incredulous that I could be the owner and asked if I could tell her any particular characteristics of the animal. I knew that Jean Sue had a notch in her ear, as this was a method of identification used by the King Ranch. So the girl, whose name was Diane Charlson, realized I had to be the true owner.

I arranged to identify Jean Sue, put my saddle in my 1965 Thunderbird, and my father came with me to the Charlson's. Their property was the image of an upscale horse farm from the Kentucky Blue Grass country. I also liked what I saw when I met Diane, who lived there with her parents. She had beautiful long, light-brown hair and a twinkle in her eyes. She was as charming and beautiful as the gorgeous surroundings. Once in front of her, I could barely speak. This lovely young woman was wearing riding pants and boots, and was pulling at my heart strings. But she was also wearing a large, expensive-looking engagement ring.

"I think you may have my horse. I mean, ah, er, possibly Jean, ah, Sue..." I stammered.

"Yes, we do have a stray horse in the barn. Let me show you" said this captivating vision as she stepped outside to the porch.

She took me to the stable. "When will you be able to come for the horse?"

Jean Sue was kicking at the sides of her stalls and in general making disturbances. "I can ride her home now," I said.

Diane was more cautious. "I don't think that's a good idea. It's already quite dark and the trails through the woods could be risky. Why don't you come back tomorrow morning?"

Now that was a good idea. I could see her again.

My father was at the wheel of my car, and when I got inside, he asked. "Well?"

"What do you mean by 'well?'

"Well, you know what I mean. How did things go with you and that lovely girl?"

"Fine."

"She is quite a lovely girl. Don't you think?"

"You betcha, Dad."

"So what are you going to do about it?"

"Well, Dad, not very much."

"Why?"

"She wore a rather large engagement ring, and it would be inappropriate for me to venture along that line."

My dad turned to me. "Francis, let me tell you something. As long as she's not married you still have the opportunity to date her."

I disagreed with him. "I certainly wouldn't mind dating her. If the opportunity ever arose, I can assure you Dad that I certainly will do it."

The next morning I was up bright and early and went to Diane's house. I spoke with her at length. I told her where I lived.

"When you bought that farm and fenced it in, my girlfriends and I couldn't cross the property with our horses as we used to."

"I'm sorry, but as you may know, I raise sheep."

"Maybe sometime my girlfriends and I could ride over and see the sheep?"

"Yes, please do!"

A few days later, Diane led her equestrian students and their horses over to my farm. I was thrilled to see her again, and proceeded to show her, and the students, my sheep and farm setup. I showed them how we lambed our ewes, how we tended them, and how we kept a herd of sheep perfect.

Diane's students must have guessed that we liked each other, which prompted some giggling. I later learned that they encouraged Diane to date me. My father also thought that was a good idea. "She's not married," he said. "All is fair in love and war."

I wasn't comfortable with that at all. It didn't seem fair to me.

Diane had developed a nice horse business. She broke Thoroughbred fillies and colts for her neighbor who was in the racing business, gave lessons, and also bought and sold horses. I liked that she was independent, loved animals, and had business savvy.

She and her students made additional visits to my farm. Eventually, one of her friends invited me to ride with them and I did so several times.

"I'd like to see you date Diane," one friend said to me on one of the rides.

"She's engaged. I can't do that."

"I don't know how long it will last with her and Jack."

Soon thereafter, on another visit from the women, one of Diane's friends took me aside. "Check out Diane's hand," she said. Lo and behold, the ring was gone.

It took me just a few moments to collect myself, and I knew what I would do now. That day I had more fun than ever before on our ride. That evening I asked Diane for a date, and she accepted with a huge smile. We saw each other as often as we could during the week and on weekends. Our common interests for animals and the outdoors drew us closer and closer. Her dream was to marry a farmer.

While we dated, Diane and her students continued to visit the farm during their lessons. Once she showed up as I was in the process of de-worming the sheep. This is not the best of jobs in sheep ranching, but necessary in keeping the flock healthy.

The sheep were Horn Dorsets that I purchased from an estate on the North Shore of Long Island. They are majestic looking, extremely hardy, and relatively easy to manage. My flock consisted of a number of ewes and one majestically horned ram. The breed represented an old line of Dorset breeding, and due to selective breeding, have long since had their horns eliminated. But that day, my flock still had them.

"Can I help with this?" Diane offered. She was familiar with the process used on horses, but de-worming sheep requires holding on to them while administering the medication.

"Yes! I would appreciate any and all help."

Diane said she would bring the sheep to my helper Ray, who was dispensing the de-worming agent. When she grabbed on to the ram, he decided not to stay around and wait to be de-wormed.

With a confident smile and determination to show me she could be as proficient with sheep as she was with horses, Diane grabbed the horned ram around his head. Instantly, with a jerk of his body, the ram took off with her holding on for dear life! Gripping on to those horns and trying to keep her feet on the ground, the ram dragged her through the grass and toward the pond. Ray and I were running to help Diane, but she held on and on, and splash! Both she and the ram were in the pond.

Diane wasn't smiling, but was dripping with water while keeping control of that ram.

"He's not going to tell me what to do!" she shouted.

I took one look at that scene and turned to Ray and said, "Any gal who can do what she just did is awesome. I am going to marry that girl. Period." I realized then that I had fallen in love with Diane. I wanted her to feel the same about me.

I now look back on the days of our courtship and have one wonderful memory after another, especially of the great discussions we had, and the great exchanges of our dreams and hopes for the future. "My dream is to have a large sheep ranch one day and market my products," I told her.

"I would love to have a horse farm and even have my own horse on the track," she said.

Diane was a quick learner and would come and help me with the sheep. In a short time she became incredibly adept at shepherding.

Like most couples, we did have our differences. One was our religious beliefs. I was Catholic and she was Protestant. She also tended to be very quiet, which was a contrast to my being outward and boisterous. Besides those two points, our similarities are what carried us along.

"How are things going with you and Diane?" my father asked me one evening.

"Just great, Dad."

One day he asked me, "How many people are there in the United States?"

"Approximately a hundred-and-seventy million.. why?"

"I guess about half are women and half are men and that gives us about eighty-five million women. That girl is one in a million. You are her one in a million too, Francis. In my view she has got to be your one in a million."

"You're right, Dad. I want to marry her."

"That's a wonderful idea. Ask her."

At that particular juncture, I had some assets, but cash was not among them. I had a deep desire to buy Diane a beautiful engagement ring.

I took a group of sheep and headed for the northwestern part of rural New Jersey and sold them at auction. With a check for the sheep in hand, I hurried to my cousin who was a diamond cutter in Manhattan's diamond center. He made a gorgeous engagement ring.

Later that week, Diane and I went to Rye Beach in Westchester County on the Long Island Sound and took a row boat out on to the water. A beautiful day with the sun shining on us, I pulled in the oars, and showed her the ring. "Diane, will you marry me?"

To my great happiness, she said a resounding "Yes!"

On one of our dates, I needed an additional witness's signature for a client's will and Diane offered to do so. While I was conferring with my client in my office, Diane waited in the reception room. After finishing up with my client Diane took me to a framed certificate in my office admitting me to the US District Court, Southern District of New York. She pointed out the authorizing signature on it and my jaw dropped! It was that of her father, my future father-in-law, Herbert A. Charlson, chief clerk of the court.

She and I decided that since we both had large families, we wanted a nice quiet wedding. I made arrangements with my local pastor at Saint Dominic's Catholic Church in Oyster Bay for permission to be married that October in Saint Joseph's Catholic Church in Chester, Vermont. We told our parents, that in lieu of a large costly wedding, we would elope to Vermont.

At the crack of dawn on October twenty seventh, 1966, Diane and I set out for Vermont. We arrived that afternoon and to our great delight the priest had everything ready. He arranged for his mother to be the matron of honor, and the local district attorney to be the best man. Within five months of our first meeting, Diane and I were married on that chilly, but sunny, fall afternoon.

Right now, I can actually smell the fragrance of getting wood for the fireplaces where we stayed as we traveled on our honeymoon. We visited farms throughout Chester, Vermont, Canada, and back to New York. It was a perfect beginning.

We returned to Mill Neck and began what would be a beautiful, successful and happy marriage digging into our respective responsibilities. Diane continued with her horses and lessons, and I with my sheep and law practice. It was interesting to see her dogs and cats playing with my dog and cat, and her large number of horses welcoming Jean Sue into their herd. We were one big happy family.

Thank you, Jean Sue, wherever you are!

Chapter 19

Wanting to Cotton in Virginia

When Diane and I relocated our lives from Long Island to Louisa County, Virginia in 1968, we experienced a culture shock. We were faced with an enormous cultural and religious difference. Keep in mind that back then, Virginia was only seven hours by car from New York and less than one hour by air - just four-hundred miles. In terms of ethnicity and religion it was as if I had landed on a different planet. It was as though we had stepped back in time, and so different from New York. I was accustomed to an abundance of Catholics, and Catholic churches, and Catholic schools, hospitals and colleges. In Virginia it was different. There were very few Catholics here when I came.

Just west of Louisa County is Charlottesville and in 1968 it was a sleepy, conservative town that encompassed the University of Virginia (technically it is in Albemarle County). Barracks Road Shopping Center had been recently built and was surrounded by farms. The area was glaringly rural. Some people were living in poorly constructed shacks with bare ground for floors in basic farm steads. Louisa County's economic structure was based on timber, except for the Green Springs area where our farm was located, which was occupied by wealthy residents with the rest of the country being poor.

Some areas in the county were big on tobacco plants, which wear out the land. Raising the same crops continuously, principally tobacco, on the same land takes a lot of chemicals and manure to replace it. That wasn't known following the Civil War and farmers kept planting until the soil was worn out, and then moved to other fields.

The Civil Rights laws of 1965 and 1968 were still "wet on the books" with serious problems between blacks and whites. The spread between wealth and poverty was enormous and a middle class was in the throes of development in Louisa County as I suppose there was in other areas of the south.

With all of this we found it very difficult to transfer a profitable law practice and a retail farm operation in such an economic climate. Diane and I tried a number of things to bring about financial success but ran into stone walls. I continued to run my law office at Oyster Bay in New York and commuted there three days a week.

On a number of occasions, I was told by locals that "your kind are not cotton to in these parts." Yes, not cotton to. I never heard such statements of hate directed to me personally. I was told that I had three strikes against me. I was: a Yankee, a Catholic, and an Italian.

I knew I wanted to educate some of the locals about what it meant to be labeled each of those things and so I began. I would take a person one on one and discuss what it meant to be a Yankee, a Catholic and Italian and understand that "our kind" didn't have horns just below the surface of our heads ready to surface at a moment's notice. I am serious about this - some really believed that "our kind" were from Satan.

Beginning with my first day on arriving in Virginia (May 10, 1968), I received a phone call from a man who sounded elderly. He welcomed me to the community and invited me to his church. "By the way, what religion are you?" he asked.

"I'm a practicing Catholic."

Immediate silence ensued and then, "Well welcome anyway," and he hung up. It took a long time for the community to accept me.

Diane and I were invited out by the local logging and lumber owner and his wife who were well to do. We attended their country club for a most enjoyable meal. We husbands sat in the front seat of their car, and Diane and his wife were in the back, The fellow turned to me and asked, "Do you know why you were invited out with us?"

Thinking the question quite odd, I said, "Well, no, why?"

"We never met a Catholic before. Now we need to meet a Jew."

I took a breath. "Well I have many Jewish friends whose company I have enjoyed over the years. My first secretary was a practicing Jew."

"Really?"

"Yes, really."

Just after Diane and I arrived, the scuttlebutt among the locals was that I had bought a big farm and was a wealthy man. In comparison to the demographics, I can see how that might have been perceived. I had been able to buy two hundred thirty five acres and later, another thousand, mostly cutover timberland. In setting up my law practice in Virginia, I hired a secretary who lived in Gordonsville, just northwest of my farm.

One day she told me that she had been to her dentist in Maryland. "I told him I was working for a lawyer who had moved to Virginia from New York, and you know what he said? He said that he had heard that the Mafia had moved in that area! He didn't even know about you, he just said that there was a wealthy guy from New York who bought land and he had to be Mafia. Can you believe that?"

It was the black community that was first to accept me to Virginia. There were several blacks who worked on the farm and word also spread rapidly that I was a fair man. After about a year, some of them came to me with their problems. "The sheriff's men are constantly pulling us over in our cars," one worker confided.

I did what I could to help. I called for a meeting in the county courthouse to speak to the black community. Citing the Civil Rights Act of 1968 to a packed audience, I told them it was a new era. "The outright prejudice against you cannot last much longer. Northerners moving to this area have no problem with blacks," I explained. "When I came here from the north I was appalled at the poverty amongst your people! Take pride in what you own and where you live."

"We don't have too much to be proud of!" shouted one man.

"Sir, God didn't make you any different than me. When you have pride in yourself you will take pride in whatever you have," I said. They all stared at me.

I continued to try to encourage them with purpose and self esteem. "Education is a major key for you to advance."

"Our schools stink!" someone said.

"So *you* work with your children. Read to them. Talk to them about what you've read and what is important. Encourage their talents and study time.

Give them hope for their own future. Teach them about responsibility. It is your responsibility to do so. Just as it is for all who are parents."

For all who attended, including me, it was a thought-provoking meeting. We were able to voice our opinions, frustrations, and hopes. The Civil Rights Act was a major change for our country, and Louisa County in Virginia was struggling to go along with it.

I then asked for a meeting with the sheriff and his deputies, and they welcomed me. When I told them of my concerns for the black community, they were met with defense.

"They're just a bunch of niggers," said one man as he crossed his arms on his chest.

"Up north, there is white trash, and there is black trash. There are law breakers of every kind everywhere. You don't pull over the whites for no reason. We are all your public -- blacks and whites. You've sworn to protect and serve all of us. It takes a lot of effort to keep somebody down. I'm just asking that you do the job that you were sworn to do for the county and make us proud."

There was a mixture of response just in body language. I could see there would be some soul searching among them, and with others, more antagonism and unwillingness to change their hearts and minds.

Oh so gradually a definite shift took place. In just over a year, blacks and whites grew more comfortable with one another in stores. Attitudes began to change and people were more relaxed and accepting, although apparently not with everyone.

Because when a young black man walked into the Louisa County Court House with a sawed-off shotgun and shot a white judge and his deputy, people began to say, "Maybe we've gone too far."

Chapter 20

The Yarn Business

At our new farm in Virginia in 1968 we had a large number of sheep and wondered what to do with the wool in our new state. Virginia was abundant with sheep and had a wool pool system for selling raw wool. Wool pools were organized by the state Agricultural Extension Service for marketing wool for the various areas of the state. Louisa County was in the central Virginia wool pool.

Each year sheep producers would consign their wool clips to their pool and the state would invite buyers to a designated place to submit written bids for the different pools. Everyone hoped that the bids would be fair and honest. It would prove not to be so as I learned from my position as head of our wool pool.

As designated captain of our selling committee I noticed that the buyers and the state agent would have a great old time drinking and having fun the night before the sale. Written bids were presented to us the next morning and strange as it may seem, the bids were as little as two tenths of a cent apart with Burlington Woolen Mills taking the lion's share of the bids and the other wool buyers divvying up the rest.

This particular year I had three-thousand pounds of my own wool consigned. The highest bid was eighteen-cents per pound. Ridiculous. I recommended rejection of the bid and committee members agreed. I had watched the market carefully and believed that wool prices would rise considerably within the next three months.

When the state agent (a so-called sheep specialist), George Allen, heard that our pool rejected the bids he approached us with the statement. You can't reject the bids. These buyers came a great distance to attend the sale. Never has a bid been rejected"

"It is about time for a rejection," I responded.

George convinced the other members to change their position and sign approval. I pulled my lot out and approached the buyer from Wellman Industries. "Am I correct in thinking that the price will triple within ninety days?" I asked. In the presence of the others he agreed that that was a strong possibility and that we did not have to take the bid. With pressure exerted upon the other members of the pool by the sheep specialist the bid was accepted, minus my wool.

Three months later I sold my wool clip to Burlington Industries at Clarksville, Virginia, for ninety cents per pound. While the wool was being examined and unloaded, an employee of Burlington suggested due to the unusual quality of the wool that my own company should produce something with it. Thus, the idea of value added to the wool - yarn - came about.

The following year our wool was processed into yarn. Diane and I packed the yarn, loaded it into our car and I took off for yarn shops in Northern Virginia and Washington DC. I returned having received ten accounts, selling a good portion of the wool, and collecting receipts many times over what I would have received selling wool through the wool pool.

And the yarn business took off.

Grandfather Enrico DeFrancesco

Maternal Grandparents Enrico and Margaret DeFrancesco

Carmine & Angela Cestari's 50th Wedding Anniversary

Carmine & Angela Cestari's 50th Wedding Anniversary

Baby Francis

Baby Francis with Pony

Francis in 1940

Sister Marie's Baptism Day - 1943

Francis with his mother and Aunt Elma

Francis as an Altar Boy on an Italian Feast Day

Francis as an Altar Boy

Confirmation Day for Francis (on the left) St. Rita's Catholic Church, Brooklyn, New York - 1948

Celebration at Sal's Restaurant Brooklyn, New York

Uncle Louie with Margaret DeFrancesco

Uncle Tom DeFrancesco in Rome - World War II

Francis as a Young Farmer Centerport, Long Island, New York - 1950's

Francis as a Young Farmer Centerport, Long Island, New York - 1950's

Francis as a Young Farmer Centerport, Long Island, New York - 1950's

Francis & Diane's Wedding Day - October 27, 1966

Scott's Birthday Party Raphine, Virginia - mid1980's

At Home in Raphine, Virginia- mid1980's L-R: Diane, Sabrina, Scott, Jen, Angelique & Francis

Glacier National Park - Montana L-R: Sabrina, Angelique, Francis, Scott, Jen

Angelique - Buffalo Gap High School, Buffalo Gap, Virginia

Francis and Diane - 2009

Sabrina. Scott. and Jen - 2009

Sheep at the Cestari Farms in Raphine, Virginia

Sheep at the Cestari Farms in Raphine, Virginia

Sheep at the Cestari Farms in Raphine, Virginia

"Heading Home" - Painting of a view at the Cestari Farms
by Virginia artist P. Buckley Moss

Editorial Cartoon 1 by Jim McCloskey The News Leader, Staunton, Virginia

Editorial Cartoon 2 by Jim McCloskey The News Leader, Staunton, Virginia

Editorial Cartoon 3 by Jim McCloskey The News Leader, Staunton, Virginia

Editorial Cartoon 4 by Jim McCloskey The News Leader - Staunton, Virginia

Editorial Cartoon 5 by Jim McCloskey The News Leader - Staunton, Virginia

Chapter 21

The Wool Fair

It was December 1970 and Diane and I were winding yarn into skeins and affixing labels to them. It was yarn that we had processed at a wool mill in New England. At this point in our lives, we were living at our first Virginia farm.

As we sat in front of the fireplace winding our skeins by hand into figure eights and placing labels on them, I thought of an idea for promoting our wool and told Diane about it. "I think we should have a wool festival when we shear the sheep in the spring. Don't you think that people would enjoy seeing how we handle the harvesting of wool?"

"Who would want to see sheep sheared?" she asked.

"There aren't many sheep people anymore, so it would be interesting especially for city folk. I think people would love to come and visit a working farm!"

In spite of Diane's protests, I moved ahead with the idea. We would process ten lambs in advance, employ a cook to roast them and sell lamb dinners. Sheep fleeces and finished yarn would be offered to the public, as well as hay rides, and exhibits. I wanted to show the sheep being sheared and drenched for external parasites, exhibit newborn lambs and whatever else we could dream up before spring.

The fair was set for the last weekend of April, and we began planning our promotion. Also, I tried to enlist the sheep expert from Virginia Tech to have other sheep people involved so that the festival would be an "industry happening" versus a Chester Farms Festival. They offered no support whatsoever, so I did it alone, along with Diane who was now a big supporter. As with many of my ideas, good or bad, she is there to assist.

We sent letters to the media and surprisingly the press was interested. It was a new idea and they took to it. A week before the festival, *The Washington*

Post wrote a long story about it on the front page of its Sunday Travel section along with several pictures and a recommendation to visit our *Wool Fair*.

Our farm at Boswells Tavern had a one-and-a-third-mile long driveway. We had visitors park their vehicles in a large clearing near the entrance and gave them a hayride into the center of the activities. We charged, at that time, an entrance fee of two-dollars and fifty cents, which included the hayride.

Local visitors poured in, as well as those from Washington, DC; Northern Virginia; and Maryland. We couldn't keep up with the crowd with the hay wagons we had. The turnaround time was too long for the massive crowd, so we borrowed a livestock trailer from a neighbor and proceeded to haul people into the activity center with it and the hay wagons. It was like hauling sheep to pasture. The crowd loved every minute of it except for one impatient woman. She wasn't going on any livestock truck and demanded of our ticket seller, Edward Marelius, that he put her on the next hay wagon. She banged on the ticket counter so hard that Ed's glasses slipped off the edge. A recent retiree from the CIA, he never once broke stride and showed great patience with all of it.

When I checked with the cook, no lamb had been sold, so I directed her to give free samples of the lamb to the public. I never realized that southerners weren't lamb eaters. We northerners eat lamb in great quantities - twenty four thousand lambs per week in New York City alone!

The free samples worked. The lambs were delicious. How could they not want it after tasting that juicy sweet meat? We sold so much that the supply was gone except for the bones. I suggested to the cook to put gravy on the bones, which still had some meat on them, and sell them too. Nothing of the lamb remained before the end of the second day of the fair.

The following April rolled around and we had another fair. A contingent from the Maryland Sheep Growers Association thought our Wool Fair idea was great and asked permission to have one in Howard County, Maryland. I told them to go ahead and that I would support their effort with the stipulation that they not use the name Wool Fair.

The next year the Association started its fair in a barn. Chester Farms (now known as Cestari Farms), participated in almost all of their Maryland sheep and wool festivals that are now held every May at the Howard County Fair Grounds. It is the largest sheep and wool festival in the United States attracting more than seventy thousand people and that number is growing.

Three years into our Wool Fair we integrated the sheep dog trials which proved to be most popular. That activity lasted until the original parties started dying off and we have not been able to put together a qualified group to hold a contest. I am open for contestants for future fairs.

The Chester Farm's Wool Fair is the oldest and the daddy of all sheep and wool festivals in the US. I say the more the merrier, for it expands the market for both wool and lamb and continues to foster our idea of educating the public about the beauty of sheep and their products -- many of which are renewable resources.

My hat is off to the sheep people in Maryland who cooperated with each other and who have done a spectacular job each year. "One for all' always does it. I wish I could have been more successful in getting Virginia's sheep people to do likewise with a large fair, but there was no interest. I was still considered a foreigner.

So each December, Diane and I still sit in front of a nice fire, and begin to plan for April's Wool Fair, as Cestari Farm will carry on that tradition for the public's enjoyment. People love to hear about something new and also enjoy their day, and passing on information about farming and my animals brings me such joy and satisfaction. I believe that teaching is my true calling. And during the seventies more, doors started to open for me to acknowledge that calling.

Chapter 22

Commonwealth of Virginia vs. Alex Poindexter

After living in Virginia just one year, I was admitted to the Virginia Bar in motion by the Lieutenant Governor of Virginia to continue practicing law at Long Island as a long-trip commuter and three days a week as a shepherd in Virginia. Soon after admission to the Virginia Bar I sold my law practice on the North Shore of Long Island and was now a committed, full-time resident of Virginia.

Louisa County proved to be a most interesting experience especially in the practice of law. As I attested to earlier, the culture and attitudes in rural Virginia in the sixties and seventies was most different from the then semi-rural North Shore of Long Island. Louisa County at the time was about fifty-one percent white and forty-nine percent black. it was a time of great adjustment for both races what with the civil rights in place and slowly being implemented in the back reaches of rural Virginia, where there was still great antagonism between the races. Initially, my law practice began slowly as the population tested my abilities as an attorney. The black population was the first to come aboard as clients and slowly the whites came.

It was February 13, 1975 and I was busy in a pasture on a tractor when Diane ran out to the field and related to me of a news report announcing Judge Stewart Cunningham, the sitting General District Court Judge, was assassinated by a young black man. The murderer was believed to be Alex Poindexter, the son of a moderately affluent saw mill operator. Judge Cunningham was white.

According to reports, the culprit, who turned out to be Alex, walked into the courtroom and with a sawed-off shotgun, blasted the judge and one deputy while they were sitting in open court. He killed the judge and wounded the deputy. As Alex was running away from the court house, he was accosted by the sheriff whom he shot and injured while making a leap to the back of the court building and on into the woods.

The state police flew helicopters and used dogs on the ground to search for the assailant, eventually locating him with attack police dogs. It proved to be a very trying time for the community, but interestingly, and as with all bad things, some good emerged.

Diane and I were quite concerned with these events. Alex had worked on our farm for a short time, and we knew him to be an intelligent and fine-mannered young man. I also knew Judge Cunningham, as he and I had some great talks when he attempted to demonstrate that prior to the Civil War, slaves in Louisa County were being given their deed to freedom in increasing numbers. He said the Civil War occurred due to hot heads on both sides. I agreed, as a student of economics, with his thesis, that slavery was becoming uneconomical and would have ceased even if there had been no Civil War. It is a fact that a young male slave was being sold for more than you could have bought a small to moderate-sized farm. We also concurred that the culture and moral ethics of the time was changing, considering slavery to be repugnant to good consciences.

One interesting thing was that the Cunninghams and the Poindexters were friends and the judge had recently been fishing at the Poindexter's pond. The acts of violence could have become a striking point of serious disobedience in this community. Diane said that if I were to be asked to represent Alex that I should consider not taking this case since both races in the community were now accepting us. It was just one or two days later, after Alex had been captured, that I was again working out in the field when Mr. and Mrs. Poindexter visited me. As I saw them approaching, I shut off the tractor and greeted them expressing my condolences for the nightmare that they were going through.

With hats in hand, they asked me to help their son. I was so taken by their collective plight. I asked them why they wanted me as Alex's attorney. They advised me that no attorney wished to represent Alex. I truly believe that everyone, regardless of his or her "obvious* guilt, has a legal and moral right to proper legal representation. Kangaroo courts, where people are not represented, are not and never should be part of the American scene. I truly felt for this troubled family and so I agreed to represent Alex.

That decision proved to be one of the most momentous ones of my life. It became the highlight of my law career, and although I would handle other murder cases and ones of public notoriety, this cause was special as it taught me several things about life. It not only became a vocal point for the public's racial attitudes, but also proved to be a means of mending between the races. If handled other than the way it was by all involved, it could have been the opposite.

The next day I visited Alex at the old state prison in Richmond. He was happy to see me. It was apparent that he had sustained minor injuries, and was severely bitten by police dogs during the course of his arrest. After I asked him some hard questions, I realized that I had to find out if there was a basis for him to plead not guilty by reason of insanity.

For anyone to be successful with such a defense, a person must come within the purview of one of two elements of the so-called M'Naghten rule. It is named for Daniel M'Naghten, an Englishman, who in 1843, was the first to be found not guilty of murder on the grounds that he was insane at the time of the act.

That M'Naghten rule states that "Every man is presumed to be sane, and ... that to establish a defense on the ground of insanity, it must be clearly proven that, at the time of committing of the act, the [person] accused was laboring under such a defect of reason, from disease of mind, and not to know the nature and quality of the act he was doing or if he did know it, that he did not know he was doing what was wrong."

I contacted Dr. Robert Showalter, a leading psychiatrist at the University of Virginia and a member of its forensic clinic. He examined Alex and I was relieved to learn that my theory of defense could work. Shortly thereafter, the Poindexter family requested that a black attorney co-counsel with me on the case. I told the family that I had no problem with that provided the other attorney agreed to cooperate in avoiding a racial confrontation.

After some debate on the name of an attorney, the Poindexters and I consented to Douglas Wilder of Richmond as co-counselor. Douglas, the grandson of a slave, was a well-dressed, suave individual and quite likable. He had been the first black elected to the Virginia Senate and subsequently the first black governor elected in the US. Still later, he became mayor of Richmond, and is now a professor at Virginia Commonwealth University's Douglas Wilder School of Government and Public Affairs, named after him.

Douglas and I hit it off right from the beginning. We worked and had lunch together throughout the Poindexter trial. I grew to admire this gentleman and to this day I have great esteem for this courageous person. During the course of these chaotic events, there was a question of my attendance at Judge Cunningham's funeral. Since I considered him a friend and colleague of the law, I requested permission from the chief judge of the circuit to attend his funeral. With his approval, I accompanied the Louisa County Bar to Judge Cunningham's funeral.

After an initial issue concerning the racial overtones of the case, I insisted that this was not a case of race but an issue solely of a disorientated individual who killed a good man. But the security was intense. Sharp shooters manned the roofs of buildings in the town of Louisa, and a considerable number of police officers were in and around the courtroom.

The trial proceeded without any troubling incidents and Alex took the stand in his own defense. He gave a chronological summary of his life with several jurors shedding tears. Alex made a superb witness, as were other defense character witnesses. The trial looked good for the defense in spite of the fact that there were thirty-six eye witnesses to the shooting that February morning in 1975.

The case was turned over to the jury and we hoped for a unanimous verdict. After several hours of jury deliberation, the jurors submitted a question to the trial judge.

What becomes of the defendant if we should find the defendant not guilty by reason of insanity?

The judge, over our strong objections, refused to answer their query and ordered the jurors to further deliberations. The answer to their question, which the jurors never heard, was that in such a scenario the defendant would have been remanded to the state mental institution and would have remained there until he was certified to be mentally competent and not be a danger to himself and others.

The jury later came out hopelessly deadlocked - eight for not guilty by reason of insanity, and four for guilty. Upon the courtroom hearing the decision of this jury, all hell broke loose with the wounded sheriff's wife pummeling me with her purse and charging me with almost getting Alex off.

Alex's parents were upset that they faced a possible new trial. The only ones pleased with this result were Douglas, me, and most importantly, the client himself. That November, the then commonwealth's attorney was defeated in his bid for reelection and was succeeded by Steve Harris who decided to retry this case.

An unprecedented motion was made by Steve to move the case out of Louisa County on the grounds that the people could not get a fair trial. This issue went all the way to the State Supreme Court, which ruled that since a defendant could be granted such a request, then why would it deny the Commonwealth from also be granted such a request.

The Poindexter family decided to remove me from the future case over strong objections from Alex. So Douglas took on the sole responsibility of a new trial, which was moved to Augusta County in the western part of the state. Its population at that time was ninety eight percent white and two-percent black. Against my advice, Douglas decided to handle the trial as conducted in Louisa. I saw this as a big problem. Blacks were not understood in that environment because there was little to no exposure between whites and blacks. It was a quick trial with the defendant found guilty on all charges. Alex, to this day, remains an inmate of the state penitentiary system.

The Louisa trial actually resulted in better relations between the races. This case inspired me to have more empathy towards clients. It also helped to establish me as a Virginian. Fewer than four years later, Diane and I and our children moved to another farm in Virginia's Augusta County. Our move was based on the fact that Augusta County, high in the Allegheny Mountains, was cool in the summers - ideal for both man and sheep. It was also a place that brought us so many more special encounters along with the risks.

Chapter 23

Have Sheep — Will Travel

While on my Long Island farm, and before I married Diane, I had a very loving tri-colored Collie named Princess. One early morning Princess awakened me urging me to get out of bed and directing me to the sheep barn. There I found one of my ewes in a difficult labor, in obvious need of assistance. I gently took the ewe and started to aid her in delivery.

I realized that she was trying to deliver twins and both were determined to come out at the same time, a physical impossibility. I also realized that my hand was too big to make much headway into her uterus, so I picked up the ewe, laid her in the back seat of my Thunderbird and headed for Farmingdale, Long Island where the state, at that time, had an agricultural research station that included sheep. I knew I could find someone to aid my ewe. It was very early in the morning with a short supply of natural light.

I arrived at the station and found someone to help me with my sheep. We both worked at helping her for some time and eventually delivered the lambs. We managed to save the ewe, but not the lambs. I cleaned up the ewe and put her back in my car for the trip back to the farm. I took the Long Island Expressway that had been built a short time before this as it reached past Farmingdale. My ewe was feeling better so she was standing up in the back seat and looking out of the window. As cars passed us, people looked in disbelief at the sight of a sheep in a T-Bird. I thought a few drivers might lose control of their cars, pointing and gawking,. That wasn't the first or last time that my sheep were great passengers!

One year, Diane and I flew out west to the Columbia Sheep Breed's annual show and sale in Montana. While there, we met a man who had Cormo sheep, a breed similar to Merino's, both producing fine wool. He told us that he would be willing to give us, like for nothing, two of his Cormo rams so that we could start producing even finer wool.

Well, this meant renting a car to drive to his Colorado ranch on mountainous and curvy roads many miles from the show. Once there to our surprise, we were facing some mighty good looking Cormos.

True to his word, we received two fine looking Cormo rams. Now what do we do with them? We put paper, burlap and whatever we could scrounge up to keep the car clean, loaded the rams in the back seat, and headed back to Montana.

Again, looks from passing motorists brought smiles to our faces. What a sight! Two rams in our rented car looking back at other cars and the world passing by. Back in Montana, we unloaded them with the help of a friend who agreed to deliver them, along with some Columbia ewes we bought at the show, to our farm in Virginia.

But then we had to return the car. It was quite an arduous job to clean and even more so to remove the odor. Diane and I were used to what we thought were pleasant smells of sheep, but we suspected that others wouldn't share our opinion. So we cleaned and scrubbed and deodorized the car. It took a lot of elbow grease to pass muster with the rental company, but we did, and we made sure the windows were opened as we did. Whew!

Columbia and Merino were the two breeds of sheep that we raised, and have continued with those breeds since the 1970s. We now also have Targhees. Prior to that, we had Horned Dorsets and Suffolks, whose fleeces are unacceptable (especially the Suffolks) to the current hand-knitting trade. Breeders paid no attention to the wool and since we could not find breeders willing to do so, we abandoned those breeds many years ago. The Dorsets have bred with the Columbias; therefore, many of their offspring's fleeces show improvement in fineness.

Internationally, wool is measured with a micrometer. The thicker the fiber is the coarser the wool. The thinner it is, the finer. The contemporary market calls for finer wool because it tends not to scratch and feels comfortable against the skin. Coarse wool is tough and durable, and has its place in carpets, rugs and some outerwear applications. We added the Merino breed to our herd in the last several years and it is the finest wool to use for garments worn against the skin.

Over the years, we have shown our Columbia sheep at shows throughout the country. As we had our children, the sheep were integrated with them into a wonderful lifestyle. Sheep are farm animals that are fun to work with and ones that children can handle and enjoy once they learn their special characteristics. Diane and I taught our children how to get sheep ready for shows. Both the children and our show stock enjoyed the process.

One year, I purchased a new one-ton dually Dodge Ram truck. It was a wide body with dual rear wheels and extended cab, and a problem from the get-go. One summer, we had planned to attend a show in Great Falls, Montana, and hooked up our trailer to the truck, loaded the sheep and children and started on our way. We were not five-hundred feet away from the farm when the truck's wiring caught on fire, burning the wiring harness.

With the repairs and replacements made, we started out again. It was smooth sailing until we reached the Badlands of the Dakotas on a hot day when the truck conked out. Here we are with four children and five sheep in the middle of nowhere when a South Dakota trooper pulled up. We advised him of our problem and he was fully aware of the cause. He said this truck model had an inherent defect. The body of the truck was too long for the gas pump to operate, especially in a really hot environment and so it would stall. "It needs an additional pump," he said.

The trooper helped us to get going and told us how to compensate until we could reach a Dodge dealership that could provide the additional pump. Stalling continued several more times in the Badlands where we stopped to enjoy buffalo burgers. Thankfully, with instructions from the trooper, we managed the situation before rolling into a Dodge dealer.

We were happy to reach Great Falls where the children handled the sheep in the show ring, assisted of course by Diane and myself. The Columbia Sheep Breeders Association was and is suited for families, and we got along well with our competing shepherds who are great people and life-long friends.

On another trip we loaded our trailer with our show sheep, and our four children and our dog in the truck to head for northern California. Passing through Utah, we were descending a mountain when the children, for the umpteenth time, decided to scream and carry on with each other challenging my driving ability and sanity.

At that point I had had it with all of the commotion and brought the truck and trailer to an abrupt stop. I ordered the kids into the trailer with the sheep thinking that this would be suitable punishment for their "crimes." They all became suddenly quiet. To my surprise they loved the idea! They were glad to be with the sheep, and excitedly jumped into the trailer with them. They waved to all the truckers as they drove by. I am sure these truckers probably realized there went a smiling driver who was fed up with all the commotion and disruption and what a great way to transport misbehaving children.

On one such trip we stopped for lunch in Wyoming where we saw a poster for an honest-to-goodness western rodeo. Off we went to the nearby event. Our children had the chance to run and tag the calves. What a good time we had watching our kids with those calves!

On another occasion we were stopped again, in South Dakota, near an Indian reservation. Diane and I had a great conversation with some of the Native

Americans who invited me to participate in their upcoming rodeo. I was humbled by their invitation but the rodeo was some days away and we had to be on our way to a sheep show.

Still another time in Montana, we visited a western ranch in connection with the Columbia show, and while riding in a wagon there, a Texas sheepman told us that he owned eight-thousand sheep. He was a great storyteller who wove stories around our surroundings about nearby rock formations with hidden Indians in attack mode against our wagon that had our children wide-eyed and entertained. He was so incredible that Diane and I were also starting to believe his tales.

We enjoyed riverboats on the northern Missouri River, visited sheep ranchers in many states, saw and participated in rodeos, hiked in the wilderness, and visited museums. We were awakened by bears raiding our food supplies in Yellowstone National Park and spent a few nights at the Big Mountain Lodge at Glazer National Park.

Those trips were educational for our kids who visited almost every state in the country, and Diane and I cherish those times with both the sheep and the children.

Chapter 24

A Shepherd Leads and Protects

I am the good shepherd: the good shepherd giveth his life for the sheep. - John 10:11

Pastore is an Italian word for shepherd. It means one who leads men or sheep. And the word pastor is derived from it. Through my experiences as a shepherd, I have seen many similarities between people and sheep. I understand this connection.

In both cases it is more effective to lead rather than to herd or push. In other words, it is best for a shepherd, of either people or sheep, to motivate his or her charges to follow.

The Bible tells us that God routinely chose shepherds such as Moses, Abraham, Jacob, and David for leadership roles. I have a theory. People are just like sheep, and if you can raise sheep, then you can lead people.

In more modern times we have Joan of Arc of France; Saint Bernadette of Lourdes, France; Saint John Bosco of Northern Italy; and the famed Portuguese children of Fatima, all shepherds. I've read that Saint Padre Pio of Southern Italy raised and cared for his father's sheep. Interesting!

Humans, like sheep, respond well to those they know and trust. A shepherd knows his sheep and his sheep know him. When a stranger comes near a herd of sheep, like people, they become suspicious and will move away from the stranger.

The Old Testament states that David was directed by God to lead the Israelites against the Philistines and was confronted with Goliath, a massive man of seven feet tall or more, who laughed at the diminutive and young David. Faced with this enormous figure, David recalled the many times he had to face wolves. He attacked his present human enemy in the same manner as when confronted with wolves that were attacking his sheep. He used his slingshot.

1 Samuel 17:40 Then he took his staff in his hand, chose five smooth stones from the stream, put them in the pouch of his shepherd's bag and, with his sling in his hand, approached the Philistine.

With wolves, a shepherd usually gets only one opportunity to slay his sheep's attacker. Shepherds of old practiced daily the art of marksmanship using a slingshot and a stone. These were lethal weapons in the hands of a skilled person.

David took careful aim at his people's aggressor. He set a stone in his slingshot and started to gain momentum and force by swinging it around and around. Faster and faster the stone whizzed around David's own head. When Goliath advanced toward the future king, David let go of the rock. With great speed and force, it made perfect contact on the giant's head. The huge Goliath stumbled and fell and Goliath was quickly discharged. With his sword, he removed Goliath's head, causing great fear among the retreating Philistines, and a victory for the Israelites.

Predators

Sheep, like people, are very vulnerable to attack from many areas. Both need good leaders to guide them through the pitfalls of life. On one particular occasion, not too long ago, a number of sheep made their way through an opening in the woods to our neighbor's lush pasture. Sheep, like people, always think that the grass is greener on the other side of the fence. Diane alerted me to the problem and I proceeded to go after the herd. As I approached, the sheep at first didn't recognize me and went into their defense posture, back to back in a circle. This is a defense mechanism that, since the time of the Romans, was very effective when approached by overwhelming force. Each individual's position is protecting the others and if held can be very efficient.

When the sheep recognized me they started moving out of their circular pattern and awaited my approach. I spoke to them in rather harsh terms, which they immediately knew meant they were in a place they were not supposed to be. I called them and they followed me one by one through the forest opening and back to their home place. I did not, nor have I ever, had to use dogs to gather the sheep. They are motivated by their shepherd who will lead them away from danger and to places of safety and good feeding. Good pastors and government leaders are expected to do likewise, to always be on the lookout for the best interests of their people.

While still in Louisa County in the mid-seventies, it was the beginning of the morning light when Diane and I heard dogs barking and sheep sounding distressed. I immediately headed in the direction of the problem, with rifle in hand, and found myself in the midst of heavy fog with the distressed sounds of the sheep getting closer and closer. I suddenly saw the source of all the noise. It was sheep in a form of a broken circle with a number of dead sheep scattered about the immediate area with three dogs attacking the sheep.

I immediately took aim, but with the overwhelming fog and the smell of mortally wounded animals, I was unable to nail down any of the attacking wild dogs. They ran off at my first approach. And then the gruesome task of counting and cleaning up the dead bodies, which numbered more than twenty heads. Upon recognizing the dead, I discovered that our prize ewe, which we could have sold for several thousand dollars, was in the lifeless pile. After patching up the injured sheep, we proceeded to run down the wild dogs. With the later assistance of the dog warden, I killed one of the dogs as it jumped, taking dead aim for me. I luckily nailed him in flight.

Shortly thereafter, the dog warden killed another one of these vicious dogs. We were never able to locate the third one, but our dog attack problems were certainly reduced with our battle that morning.

We were now faced with the challenge or determining how to keep predators from the sheep. Diane and I came to the conclusion that the Romans of old seemed to have solutions to most problems and so the research began. Our search led us to the old proverb: fight fire with fire. In other words, fight wild dogs with good guard dogs, and so the introduction of a Great Pyrenees dog into our family. The breed, used for hundreds of years by shepherds in France and Spain, produces large dogs.

Our first one was a one-hundred-fifty pound male with a thick white coat. We named him Caleb and what a guard dog he was. With his presence, our wild dog problem literally disappeared. He would lie down in the pasture with the sheep instinctively accepting him and knowing he was one of them or rather part of the good shepherd contingent.

Caleb responded to his responsibilities with gusto. He loved his charges and they him; however, when the ewes had their lambs and Caleb wanted to mother them, the ewes let him know from the start that he was not to bother the lambs. A few butts by the ewes got the message across real fast. We also learned that the Great Pyrenees breed is not only a protector of sheep, but also a defender of our family.

When our children started to come along, Caleb, sensing the need of our children's protection, would run back and forth from the sheep pasture to the house not knowing where he should be. On one occasion, Diane and I drove to town to get some supplies and left our children with Maria, one of our employees. We had set up a small cyclone fenced area for the children. When we returned that day, Maria was still upset after a harrowing experience with Caleb. It seemed that our daughter Jennifer started to cry while in the fenced play area and when Maria ventured forth to pick her up, Caleb jumped on her placing his huge front paws on her shoulders, and growled into her ears. She quietly and very slowly put Jennifer down, at which point she stopped crying and Caleb removed his feet from Maria's body and wagged his tail in response.

We had ocher less-harrowing experiences with Caleb and later other family sheep-dog members, but these dogs taught us lessons that helped us co-exist with this fine breed. They are big lovable animals and can easily respond to danger.

Shepherds are constantly on alert to fight off predators of their sheep. At one time, sheep were well protected by nature with horns, but man selectively bred horns out of sheep, although some breeds, such as Merino and Jacob, still have them.

But horns can be dangerous to a handler. My grandfather Cestari had a large number of goats on Long Island. One day, while handling one of the does in heat, a buck took after my grandfather, and caught him against the barn ramming him with his horns. What saved my grandfather was the fact that the buck's horns were long and curled towards his back, which prevented him from bending his head down far enough to pierce my granddad. When my granddad got away with his life, he took his rifle and shot the buck. When an animal gets the taste of attacking a human, it's time for that animal's demise. I have been attacked by rams and bucks and they met their Creator real quick.

We once had a ram named Charlie. He was overly protective of the ewes and began to have tendencies towards ramming. Charlie didn't have horns, and was not so aggressive that he couldn't be controlled with a broom when he started up. After Diane and I were married, he had an eye on her, and she used a broom to settle him down. One day, we heard a loud repetitive noise coming from the barn. Charlie had found the broom and was ramming, ripping, and urinating all over it. It was destroyed. Nothing was left for Charlie to fear.

My point is that shepherds have to be leery of wild dogs, coyotes, wolves and mountain lions. Before there were guns, sling shots were used to kill invaders. Shepherds became experts at this because they only had one chance to do the job.

In our research, Diane and I found that the Romans of old discovered the Tibetan Mastiff and developed the Great Pyrenees dog breed. They became a permanent fixture with the Italian shepherds and were pastured in the Pyrenees and Alp mountain regions of the Roman Empire. The Roman shepherds placed hard leather collars around the necks of their dogs with spikes protruding to the outside of the collar. This protected the dog from attacks by bears and wolves, the main predators of sheep. When a predator tried to attack the dog it would go for the neck, its most vulnerable part. The predator would then be greeted not only by the dog's huge mouth, but also an unpleasant stab from the implanted spike. The predator would flee not wanting to come after the sheep again, as the Pyrenees resemble the sheep.

Today, we shepherds are faced with new challenges in raising sheep. Coyote, an animal similar to the wolf, but more reticent and less bold, smaller in stature, and originally from the west, are now living all over the United States. They cause considerable chaos and destruction not only to sheep, but also to calves and fowls, driving many ranchers out of business due to great loss of their livestock.

Another challenge on the horizon is the wolf, an animal full of ancient lore but long disappearing from the lower forty-eight states. A beautiful animal, and extremely intelligent, the wolf is bold and seriously dangerous to livestock and even children. For many years, wolves were a rarity in the continental United States except when they would occasionally come down from Canada.

Several years ago, the United States government, and in particular its National Park Service, decided that visitors to our national parks needed the experience of seeing wolves in their natural environment. So in 1996 it decided to relocate fourteen wolves from several wolf packs at the Yellowstone National Park in western Montana. The National Park Service said that the wolves would remain in Yellowstone, but anyone knowing the wolf's nature knew otherwise. The once non-existent wolf problem is now becoming much more prevalent, as wolves living throughout the west are now moving to the Midwest. Those in the east expect wolves to invade within three years as the original packs are multiplying at a great rate.

As with the coyote, we do not need the added predator of the wolf. Don't be suckered in with the wolf's beauty. The animal is dangerous and deadly.

Bears can also be a problem in shepherding navigation. Back in the mid-1980s when we had our sheep operation in Raphine, located in Virginia's Augusta County, we discovered during a bad snow storm that ten of our finest rams were missing. Diane and I rode up the mountains on horseback to track the missing sheep. We found our ten rams killed and covered with leaves and snow. After a careful investigation, we concluded that a marauding female bear had visited us.

Representatives from the Virginia Game and Inland Fisheries trapped the bear in a humane cage along with her two cubs. They were quickly transported to wilder parts of West Virginia.

Today, predator control has been broadened to include the anti-predator's arsenal including the donkey, the llama, good rifles in the hands of marksmen and, of course, the traditional sheep dog, the Great Pyrenees. Several other anti-predator breeds of dogs such as the Komodo, Kuvasz, Anatolian, and Akbash are all competent at what they do, but with varied personalities in their relationship to man. As such, they require careful selection and observation.

Those who have not experienced having their sheep attacked might surmise that my attitude toward predators is harsh. I love animals and I wish them no harm, but when my sheep are attacked, killed or maimed, I become less sensitive to the beauty of the predator and more sympathetic to the mauled or dead sheep. After working so hard to feed, care for, and raise these animals only to wake up one morning to find them a bloodied mess beyond recognition, I became a changed person.

Chapter 25

Sheep Taking a Bow

In the late seventies, I came up with the idea of training three sheep (yes, sheep are capable of being trained), fitting them, and making arrangements to visit stores to promote sheep and wool. I wanted to partner with a major quality store, so I contacted the Belk-Legget chain, (now Belk, Inc.) whose headquarters is in Charlotte, North Carolina. This chain sold, and still sells fine products - mainly clothes, and at the time, a line of quality knitting yarns.

Mr. White, one of the chief buyers for the company, was most impressed with my concept and proposal to bring three trained and trimmed sheep to the Belk-Legget stores and agreed to the idea. I readied Chester, Me Too, and Ewe Too for our trips by washing them and trimming their fleece. Each was fitted with a halter and I walked them, first individually and finally as a team, one following the other.

We had a two-horse trailer that Diane and I made comfortable for the sheep, hooked it up to our truck and we were set to go. The invitations to bring the sheep to the Belk stores started to come in slowly at first as there was some strong hesitation on the part of many of the store managers as to the whole idea of bringing three, two-hundred pound sheep into their stores.

Before our event date, managers would display proper and sufficient advertisements to bring customers in. Each store would also purchase a previously agreed-on amount of our yarn and have it on display when I arrived with appropriate signage around. I didn't charge for my time or travel expenses, as I thought my sheep and I would produce lasting results for our yarn business.

Chester was a purebred Columbia ram, Me Too was a black-horned Karakul ram, and Ewe Too was a ewe of the Columbia breed. When we arrived with them at a store, I set up a pen inside where the three would stand on waterproof canvas and straw bedding, with water pails, feed and hay. We provided literature about our farm and yarn products and I spoke to the customers about sheep and wool - particularly Cestari wool yarn.

Our first store visit was a smashing success, even though there were other companies featuring their products simultaneously with our in-store promotion. I didn't figure on the hitching on to the "back of the sheep" promotions by other companies, but as it turned out it was a great win for all.

As word got out about how well our first visit went, we started to get many requests and at times I would wind up doing two promotions a day for Belk-Legget, going from store to store adjacent to one another.

Belk-Legget started to increase the size and frequency of its ads about the sheep appearances. In addition to receiving calls from newspapers, which featured our store visits in their publications, I made guest appearances on television shows.

On one occasion, Frankie Lane, the famous singer and I were both guests on a call-in show at the same time. Of course, I took the sheep with me and on that particular TV program, the sheep had more calls than Frankie! He was such a good sport about it and commented on the show that he had many public appearances but he was "never upstaged by some sheep," which brought laughs from everyone. While everyone was enjoying the laughter, the three sheep joined in with a series of baas. More laughter!

Each store had different challenges we needed to overcome about setting up the pen, and I would work it out with the sheep in tow. Eventually Chester required only one lead shank with Me Too and Ewe Too following him closely. We were a team and people enjoyed the sight.

There was only one misstep at a store. A woman kept annoying Me Too who would then butt his head against the shepherd's crook, which I had always stood up as a symbol. The crook fell, hitting the woman on her lip that gave off some blood. She had very poor-looking teeth, and even though they weren't damaged in that incident, Belk worked it out with her. She was actually planning to have all of her teeth pulled anyway and the store provided her with dentures. I thereafter made sure that no one teased the sheep.

On another occasion at the old Belk store in Fredericksburg, Virginia, I had the choice of either taking the sheep in the elevator or walking them up the stairs to the second floor where the yarn department was located. This was a first for the elevator and the sheep acted just great following me wherever I walked with my shepherd's crook in hand. Their first elevator ride was uneventful.

To save expenses on overnight trips I would sleep in the trailer with Chester, Me Too and Ewe Too. Chester slept closest to me as he was the biggest sheep and his fleece kept me warm. They really were great companions.

In addition to visiting some forty Belk stores encompassing three-hundred miles in less than a year, I also did a promotion for Bloomingdales at its new and beautiful Flat Rock, Maryland, store. There, I was directed to walk the sheep through the imported fine glassware department, where the narrow aisle was a challenge. I questioned the advisability of passing through such expensive glassware but was reassured about the liability. I held my breath and said my prayers as the sheep followed me without hesitation and without moving a glass.

That promo was in late November, and about three hours into our visit, the general manager of the store came to me saying that as a result of our sheep visit, the mall's sales increased twelve percent and Bloomingdale's sales were up more than twenty percent.

"Mr. Chester, I want you and your beautiful sheep to work along Santa Claus for the next few weeks. Name your price." he said.

I didn't take his offer. which was foolish of me, saying I wanted to promote our yarn. He advised me to forget the yarn and work the sheep in visits.

After all of this work, the Belk chain closed its yarn departments a short time later, and so did my yarn promotions with Belk. So I began to market with several small independent yarn shops to great advantage. One invitation came from the Ladies Yarn Shop on Eighty Fourth Street and Broadway in Manhattan.

Before arriving at their shop, I called the police precinct covering that area to ask for permission to park some place on Broadway. The officer who answered said, "You are bringing sheep to a store on Broadway? Buddy, you can park wherever you want and I will advise my officers to leave you be. I expect crime to decline fifty percent due to your visit. Have fun!"

And so I parked on Broadway and walked the sheep to the store. We were the object of surprised looks, happy comments, and laughter. Chester, Ewe Too, and Me Too had visits from nearby wealthy tenants who brought their expensive dogs to see sheep for the first time. We even had press coverage in the *New York Daily News*. It was the Friday after Thanksgiving and our picture and story were on the paper's front page together with centerfold pictures, plus a full story for its circulation of several hundred thousand.

That was great exposure and a fun time for me going to the stores and talking to customers. Despite the cost in time, travel and more, this publicity venture created many joyous memories. It is one of the best ideas we ever took on!

Chapter 26

Wool Mill # 1

In the fall of 1980, Diane and I moved our family from Louisa County to a beautiful antebellum farm in Raphine, Virginia. It was a complex move hauling our sheep, horses, dogs, cats, goats and other of God's creatures on the eighty-one mile trip.

At this point we found it very difficult to get a timely turnaround of our sheared wool from mills. Our new farm had a large building on it, so I decided to build my own wool mill. When Diane and I learned about a wool mill in Philadelphia that was going out of business, we headed north to look over its equipment. We liked what they had, purchased it, and had the equipment moved and reassembled at our Raphine farm. I hired a husband and wife team to put the machines together, and more people to manage sales reps. We were off and running with a yarn business and mill to boot. It was an exciting time.

Then something really wonderful happened which actually ultimately undermined the whole operation. I received a call from the executive director of the International Wool Bureau whose US office was in New York City. He suggested that I submit our yarn in competition that summer. It was 1983. With the submission came a big surprise - we won the Showcase Award of *Women's Wear Daily*, known as the retailers' daily newspaper. With that came recognition, and jealousy.

About a week after learning of our award, we received a call from the director of the wool bureau who indicated that Burlington Industries was most distressed by our win, suggesting that a small operation such as ours should not be the recipient of any award. When they told him that they were the largest wool operation in the world, he said he responded with, "Quality over corporate wins."

Thereafter, strange things started to occur: my bank demanded that I sell my yarn through a distributor, wool pools wouldn't sell their wool without costly up-front procedures, and sheep farmers were threatened if they attempted to sell their wool directly to me. The nightmare began.

To satisfy my bank, I reluctantly turned my sales over to Bernat, a yarn distributor in Uxbridge, Massachusetts. I decided on that company because it was run by a wonderful woman, Mrs. William Bernat, a great yarn designer and businesswoman.

With immense anguish I had to terminate my sales force. Within six months, Mrs. Bernat sold her company to a French conglomerate which went ahead to deep six my yarn since they already had a competing yarn line in Ireland. Bernat's sales force told my accounts that my company was "going out of business…going bankrupt" and continued to sell the Irish line. Our sales plummeted. Many shops where we did a great volume of business and were loyal to the United States were dropped.

It was a disaster.

Attempts to get the Justice Department to intervene went unheeded even though a representative admitted that what occurred was wrong. Due to political consideration, nothing could be done. I was on my own.

I chose to circle our wagons and fight back. I conducted a voluntary auction and sold the mill equipment, some of the farm equipment, and much of the yarn inventory to pay off the bank's liens. Even the building that housed the wool mill was sold. We were able to save the sheep and the main farm by getting the bank out of the picture. As a last resort, I did try to save the wool mill building. I had Diane's cousin, Bob, bidding on it when a chiropractor, who was driving by, saw the crowd, stopped and asked what was going on. He proceeded to outbid Bob who wanted to save the mill. It was meant to be that way.

Of course, this was a very sad time for everyone involved. As the farm tractor was being sold, my son cried. "This is the tractor you taught me to drive," he said and choked back tears.

"I'm so sorry. We have to do this. One day we'll get another, and you'll already know how to drive it."

Losing my employees was painful as well. When it was all done, I promised that we would rebuild our business from scratch. It was just a few years later when I would be able to keep that promise.

There was a group of people from West Virginia who wanted our wool mill in the worst way and even tried to get our customer list without success. When I had the volunteer auction, they showed up to get the equipment, which we worked so hard to restore.

During the auction, one of my clients, a good and faithful friend, Mary Shomo, was determined that the assemblage from West Virginia or others would pay a high price for the items. I tried to prevent Mary from getting involved as I was concerned for her getting stuck with things she could never use. But she insisted and was a great morale booster for our family at a time of great embarrassment. She kept the prices from being too low.

There is a very interesting thing that can be said about my losing the wool mill. Every person or company who was underhanded and unethical and bought equipment, wool mill property, eventually paid dearly for it.

For instance, the West Virginia people bought the wool mill equipment and hired a local farmer to load the equipment onto uncovered flat bed trailers. The farmer hooked a chain to the spinning frame and jerked it out and it went crashing onto the ground by the loading dock. The machine was broken into hundreds of pieces.

The rest of the equipment was loaded onto three uncovered flat bed trailers. That night a terrible hurricane came in and drenched the equipment, ruining all of it. Two trailers broke down, never to reach their destination. The third trailer had to go around Wheeling, West Virginia, because of extensive flooding. The equipment was unloaded in a wooded clearing, and to this day is rotting away.

The chiropractor who bought the mill property wound up getting a divorce and lost the property.

The old Burlington Mills (not the one carrying the name today, which is privately owned) had a hostile takeover costing it millions of dollars, and had to lay off ten-thousand people. The person attacking Burlington was Canadian and owned Federated Department Stores. He wanted a mill to have a complete vertical operation: from mill to department stores. He was unsuccessful.

I called the folks at Burlington and suggested that what goes around comes around. You reap what you sow. Burlington would eventually go bankrupt and a private party bought part of it.

As a last ditch effort to save the mill, I contacted the Justice Department in Washington, DC, and met with three assistant general attorneys collectively who said they were aware what was going on. When I suggested that it was illegal monopoly tactics, they agreed.

"Can I expect criminal actions?"

"No, you're on your own," said the one with higher authority.

After that, I received anonymous information on the situation from different parts of the country. The only identification available was a post office location. I could not even get a private law firm specializing in monopolies to help me. I was truly on my own. After the auction, I paid off my loans except for the mortgage with Farm Credit on the unaffected main farm and of course, some residual bills. I built a small building on the farm and put my law office into full gear and the clients came. Along with that cash flow to pay my remaining bills, I was fortunate to become the attorney on a tragic and difficult death case resulting in a large fee which further helped to save the family financially.

Chapter 27

My Life as a Professor

Teaching is the profession that teaches all the other professions. ~Author Unknown

Let me say right up front that teaching is a wonderful profession and I have the highest opinion for good teachers. Some of them, like shepherds, were born with the innate ability to teach. Others just need the training to be good educators. All instructors need to enjoy enlightening others to be successful at the profession. I enjoy teaching. It has become one of my passions.

How I got my start in teaching was purely by accident. In the early eighties I was invited by the Entrepreneurial Club at the University of Virginia's Commerce Department in Charlottesville to give a talk on my experiences in the world of business. As a result of that successful lecture, I received a phone call from the academic dean at Piedmont Community College, also located in Charlottesville, Virginia. This is a two-year college program encompassing many academic and technical fields in which many students elect to take their first two years of college in the community college arena for several possible reasons. It is much less expensive, especially since you can live at home and travel short distances to class; the more timid students are able to break into the college culture; and students usually have good teachers who often have extensive business and/or professional experiences.

The dean told me that his full-time professor was going on his seventh year stint with an oil company operation as a consultant and he needed someone to handle his assignments for that year. I accepted, and was required to teach four courses in economics; however, I would be considered a part-time replacement.

This was my first adventure into a formal teaching program. My developed techniques in trying cases and ease at giving lectures and speeches helped me, so I had little difficulty in coming to the "plate." If student evaluations are any testimony, my first year at teaching was quite successful.

Teaching proved to be most enjoyable for me, and I made new friends amongst the students and faculty. I still practiced law, ran the farm and wool mill, allocating the appropriate time and needed attention to wearing a specific hat for each of my careers.

I enjoyed the experience so much after that one-year assignment, I sought more part-time commitments. My next adventure at teaching was at Southern Seminary College in Buena Vista, Virginia. At the time, this was a two-year private women's college, which has since changed to a co-ed university owned and operated by the Mormon Church.

Initially, it was a pleasant experience. I met some real fine people. My subject for instruction this time was constitutional law, in which I find great interest.

During the course of teaching, I cited many US Supreme Court cases. One that especially drew intense interest from the class was *Roe vs. Wade*, which had been decided by that court in 1973, just nine years earlier. The Supreme Court overturned a Texas law and made abortion legal in the United States.

From time to time students would ask for my own opinion on decisions of cases. Professors should always give the arguments of both sides to any issue especially when discussing court cases. Once that has been accomplished, a professor should be free to expound and explain his or her own view about the arguments. The *Roe vs. Wade* case proved to be especially interesting to the young women in my class. I gave both arguments of the case and when asked for my opinion, I told them that I was a practicing Catholic who believed in all the principles and dogmas of my church. I told them I opposed abortion, as I truly believed that it was the taking of an innocent human life.

I explained that, *As a practicing attorney, I feel it was a bad decision without any constitutional reference at all. Many in the legal profession find serious fault with the Roe decision because there is no place in the Constitution that permits it. Further, the Constitution does not give the feds authority over abortions."

"It has always been a state issue, usurped by the feds with this decision, However, does the reference in the Preamble to 'promote the general welfare…' mean we providing for the general welfare by taking an innocent life? Is killing more than fifty million little babies(and they are little babies in the wombs of their mothers) more than were killed during World War II providing for the general welfare?" I asked.

There were a lot of serious discussions about this case and that is exactly what the role of a professor should be: generate thought and reasoning. Well, one student said she was a Catholic and believed in abortion (In my opinion, one is not a practicing Catholic if one believes in abortion).

I told her as a student she had a right to her own views. I was there to facilitate sound reasoning.

She, along with the other students, took the final exam. She received a B and filed a protest with the dean who called me on the carpet. This academic dean was extremely liberal and a feminist of the first order. She had me review the exam to see if my prejudice against abortion tainted my ability to judge this student's test. I did as asked and I came up with the same final grade of B.

I pointed out to the dean where the student went wrong and established the grade. Shortly after that incident, my contract was not renewed. This generated serious protests among the faculty without any degree of change.

In September, I received an invitation to the annual president's reception for the faculty. I called the president and advised her that I was not reappointed. She was shocked but it was too late to do anything about it. I had already accepted a contract with Blue Ridge Community College and taught there for several years without any problems.

In speaking with other professors, the type of reaction to voicing my opinion at Southern Seminary is more commonplace than the public can imagine. The left leaning liberal bent in this country is literally controlling the majority of the campuses today. It is difficult for an honest, conservative-thinking professor to secure a position at these campuses let alone tenure. I believe that this is having deleterious effects on the minds of our future leaders since the colleges and universities provide most of the leadership positions in the professions and businesses. This, in my opinion, is dangerous. At the very least, students should be exposed to both sides of issues and truth will emerge.

It was ten years after Diane and I had moved to Virginia (and still had not uncovered the missing thesis entitled *Insanity and Moral Responsibility*) I decided to go back to St. John's graduate school for my master's degree - this time in political science. I was relieved to be accepted into the program at their Hillcrest, Queens County campus on Long Island, still a part of New York City. I was told that if I would successfully complete four more courses, I would be granted my degree.

And thus with great determination, I started a major commute from our farm in Augusta County, Virginia, to New York City. Early each Wednesday I took a train from Charlottesville, Virginia, to Washington, DC, then to Pennsylvania Station in Manhattan, where I would catch the subway to Queens, Long Island. After my early evening classes, I would sleep in a nearby motel and return to school on Thursday. After more classes on Friday, I would return home late

Friday evening. It was so pleasing to be back in the academic environment with its mental challenges and I thrived.

While at St. John's, another teaching position presented itself to me in an unusual way. My courses were populated, for the most part, with Foreign Service and diplomatic personnel from all over the world. The United Nations, located in Manhattan, isn't far from the St. John's campus via subway.

One evening towards the end of completing my course requirements, the professor came to me before class and suggested that I teach the group that evening. Without hesitation, I agreed to the challenge and the professor announced to the attending diplomats that I was going to give the lecture. He proceeded to take a back seat in the room while I taught.

I must have been a successful lecture because that professor suggested that I give college lectures at a Catholic college in Front Royal, Virginia, which was located less than two hours from my farm. At the time, Christendom College was a four-year institution, and in its early days of development, had only had a few graduations.

My professor contacted Dr. William Luckey, head of the political science department. His call resulted in my teaching at Christendom for fourteen enjoyable years in a conservative environment that suited me to a tee.

Subjects in economics and law were a wonderful challenge. Because of my business and professional experience, I was often sought for advice and I was happy to oblige. On one occasion I was taken aside by an economics' student. "I would like your opinion about a vocation I'm interested in. I've discovered that I enjoy the brick laying business. I would like to be a brick layer. Is this foolish?" he asked.

I told him, without hesitation, that he should go into a field that he would enjoy. "Bricklaying is a very noble profession requiring the use of many talents such as math, chemistry and patience. Go for it!" I said. He did and eventually owned his own company.

In addition to my position as a part-time professor, I directed the political science field trip program. In that capacity, I took my students to see the United States political governmental system at work. Over the years, my students and I made frequent visits to the United States Supreme Court to visit the likes of Justice Antonin Scalia and Justice Clarence Thomas who graced us with their extensive comments about the functioning of the U.S. Supreme Court. Through this association, I came to personally know Justice Antonin Scalia whom I greatly admire.

Students learned by sitting in on oral arguments of this court, saw the judges' library, and listened to my war stories about the practice of law. My actual teaching in this capacity was an enjoyable occasion. I didn't have to be concerned if someone didn't like what I was discussing. I was a conservative in the midst of a sea of conservative thinkers.

Educational institutions are not always out in the open community. At one point, I was asked to teach at two Virginia state prisons. One was formerly a mental institution built in Staunton during the 1840s and 1850s, and the second was a more modern prison located in the extreme outskirts of a little town called Craigsville. Both had difficulties recruiting teachers. I believe that people get intimidated with prisons, and having been used to visiting clients in prison, I did not have a problem going to one.

At the Staunton facility, which has since been made into condominiums, I met an inmate who was serving a life sentence. This man held two masters degrees - one in nuclear submarines and another in nuclear engineering. A quiet person in his late fifties, he always excelled in the classes I taught. I was not aware of the reason for his incarceration.

He had a great mind, and wanted to keep it stimulated. I always wondered why something couldn't be done to activate his talents. There are many like him in prisons. This man could have been productive in his field, and probably would have made a huge income on the outside, but instead, his life was confined to jail. What a pity!

The constitutional law course seemed to provoke much talk in my classes. One pupil, a large black man, became aggravated when the subject of the Dred Scott U.S. Supreme Court decision was discussed. This famous 1857 decision declared that slaves and their descendants were not protected by the Constitution and could never be US citizens.

Obviously a terrible decision, but it was, nonetheless, a major legal chapter in the history of our country. When the subject of this case was introduced in class, this man became extremely belligerent and stood up, clenched his fists at his side, and showing anger in his whole body, told me he wasn't going to listen "to no slavery case."

"Please sit down. I am going forward with this important case," I said.

He continued his ranting and became a real handful. Correction officers, stationed outside the room heard his loud epitaphs and burst in to remove him permanently from the classroom. This was an unpleasant, but rare, encounter for me because most of the inmates were appreciative of my being there. In that same class was a student who was convicted, while serving in the

US Navy, of a double murder in a bar in Norfolk, Virginia. I never had a problem with him and he was a diligent "for-lifer" student.

Chapter 28

More Interesting Cases

One time I was approached by a man who was charged with voluntary manslaughter of his infant child. The charge was shaken baby syndrome. These are very difficult cases because they are an exceptionally intense and trying situation with jurors ready to throw the book at any accused defendant. Passion plays a big part in the proceedings, even though the courts try to be impassioned.

In investigating the facts of a case, I often go back to the scene of the events and look over the area and the things that affected it. It's amazing at what can be ascertained by an on-site visit. I encourage attorneys on both sides of an issue, civil or criminal, to see the place where an alleged crime took place.

My visit to the place of the child's death was a small, older home, where a young couple lived. The neighbors' houses were close on either side. My observation showed to me that the love of this couple was one sided, in which the husband greatly loved the mother of the deceased child. The mother seemed dispassionate towards her husband, and towards their older child. The investigation indicated that she was furthering her education and loved office work, and considered herself above her husband, who was a mechanic.

I determined early in my analysis that the father did not kill his child. It had to be someone else. The time of death was important, but the pathologist could not pinpoint it. This left a span of several hours, in which there had been contact with the child by both the mother and father.

When the father came home from work, the child was sleeping, and his wife left the house. The father noticed that the child was lethargic but wasn't concerned until the child failed to awaken. He called the rescue squad, and the child was dead.

The father was charged because he was on duty during the child's death. I visited the state's medical examiner's office in Richmond, Virginia, and learned more about the events leading up to the child's death. The pathologist allowed me to inspect the little brain of this lovely child. It was evident that the brain sustained several contusions resulting in bleeding.

It was clear that someone lost patience with the child due to possible crying and shook the child to stop the crying. When the head of the child was flipping from back to front in a series of quick shakes, it caused lethargic reactions and subsequent death.

I was convinced that my client did not kill the child, and suspected the mother, who was a very tense person. My client had a quiet and loving nature. When the jury trial started, I wanted to seriously question my client's wife about her involvement. I told him my theory that his wife lost her cool, picked up the child while screaming, shook the infant, and placed the child back in the crib. When my client came home, she left to go out.

He did not want his wife questioned. He said he would take any of the consequences. "I am innocent. If she did it, I will pay the price, not her." I appealed to my client the best I could with the proverbial hands behind my back.

The jury came back with a modified verdict and gave my client one year in jail, versus the thirty years he could have received. It was obvious that the jury, like me, had doubts.

The press was all over me. They said I got a murderer, a child killer, off. I knew better. As it turned out, his wife was having an affair with a married man, before and after her husband's trial. I felt some vindication of my theory.

Another case involved a young man who was charged with assaulting his father-in-law. I was able to keep him from receiving a felony conviction, which entitled him to have guns. At the conclusion of the case the sheriff came over and requested that I get my client to surrender his gun. I submitted the sheriff's request to my client, who turned to me and asked, "Am I required to do so?"

"No," I said.

"No," he told the sheriff.

The sheriff looked at me. "You will not see the end of this."

"My client, under the law, has a right to his guns," I said.

I left the courthouse feeling that I got my client off of a possible felony conviction. About three months later, I picked up a newspaper with a headline proclaiming that a man was shot and killed by his son-in-law. Yes, it was my client who shot him, using the same gun he threatened his father-in-law with three months before.

I investigated the matter and found that my client approached his father-in-law, who was sitting in his car in front of the court house, and shot him to death. My client then walked over to the sheriff, handed him his gun and said, "I will not need this anymore."

After this killing, I did not handle anymore criminal cases for awhile. I felt partly responsible for the aftermath. I used my skills to the point that my client was able, under Virginia law at that time, to keep his weapon. I refused to take criminal cases until one day one of my wool mill employees came to me and pleaded for me to represent him in a grand larceny charge.

"I don't do criminal cases," I stated.

He was pleading. "Please. Please. You are the only one I can trust."

I reluctantly took the case. The trial was held in Lexington, Virginia, and during the proceedings, the prosecution made a blunder and I jumped on it. I made the necessary motion to dismiss the charge. It was granted and my client walked. As I was leaving the courthouse, the owner of the stolen car followed me for three blocks yelling, "It's your fault that he walked free!"

I finally stopped, put down my file and turned to the screamer and said, "Buster, I represented the defendant who was entitled to an attorney. I am not supposed to be the prosecutor too. If you disagree with the decision of the court, then vote the prosecutor out of office." Thereafter, I did take criminal cases.

Our judicial system is based on an adversarial system pitting one side against the other. In theory, when you have such a system, truth emerges but in actuality that is based on equally experienced and intelligent lawyers supported with adequate financial and evidentiary resources. Thus, sometimes innocent people get convicted and guilty persons walk.

Every person charged with a crime, carrying a possible incarceration term is, under the Sixth Amendment to the Constitution of the United States, entitled to be represented by an attorney. However, everyone is also entitled to represent oneself. All are considered innocent, of any criminal charge, until proven guilty. This is pure theory. Just try to stand pat and do nothing to force the state to prove the guilt of an accused individual. The overwhelming result is, that innocent or not, you will be found guilty. You must have financial and evidentiary resources together with a capable lawyer to have good chance of success.

Chapter 29

Wool Mill # 2

After the close of our first mill, I continued in the yarn business by having my own wool processed by a mill in New England.

In time, I began to be concerned with wool mills closing down in the United States and moving to China and India and other points east. I thought, *what will happen if my US out source closed its doors? What would I do?* I started to think about that and remembered my first experience owning and operating such a mill. I also recalled my promise to rebuild the mill.

So slowly I started to buy one machine, then another, and then I became serious about it and visited "friendly" banks for capital. I went to twenty-two banks and every one of them turned me down saying, "Why do you want to do such a crazy thing when all the textile mills are closing and going overseas?"

One bank manager even suggested that I sign myself into an insane asylum. Thus, there was no capital forthcoming from the banks. I did what I had done in the past. I relied on my cash cow, the law practice for the needed money. It was going to take longer but the alternatives, venture capitalist or partners, were unacceptable. In both cases, I would be losing control of my company.

I realized that I would need patience as it was going to take time. So gradually I acquired more machines and started the task of assembling the equipment. I could not afford new and efficient machines. Just one fifty-nine foot long card that starts the yarn process would cost two million, five hundred thousand dollars. And that was one for machines from Italy, Germany or Japan.

So I acquired old, but still running, equipment and was determined to modify and reinforce (for the most part) the quality of the machinery. Manufactured in the 1940s and 1950s, they were still operational. The machines were mostly built of cast iron, so we used a local quality steel fabrication company to make replacement parts, and extras, when there wasn't a spare. The result was stronger built and more efficient equipment.

Wherever we could make the machines more effective, we did. All of them were engineered and manufactured in the US using American labor. They are so good that after fifty or sixty years of constant use, they are still running, and when we repair and start them, they purr like new. I'm told by machine experts that, with love and care, and lots of oil and grease, they could be running for yet another fifty or sixty years.

The engineering that went into planning these machines is astonishing. The newer ones used in wool mills are products of the same engineering concepts that go back one-hundred-fifty years, except that now, computers are part of their mechanism instead of manual settings and controls.

Two engineers from Grumman Aircraft Corporation, who worked on the NASA program, heard about my antique machines and were curious about them. The gentlemen stayed in our mill for more than two hours marveling about the engineering contained in their original construction, especially that fifty-nine foot long wool card. I questioned them about their interest, which seemed elementary compared to the complexities of the space program. These aeronautical engineers told me that my wool cards were more complex and more of a marvel than any part of the space program.

In addition to searching for, acquiring, relocating and rebuilding these machines, we needed experienced help in running.and maintaining the devices.

With our country being obsessed over outsourcing our manufacturing base - textiles and steel especially - we have and are dismantling the infrastructure of these industries. What am I talking about? Every industry has supporting companies that supply the services and products needed to keep that industry going. Take textiles. You need dyers and their equipment, wool-washing fiber facilities, parts and replacement wire and ancillary supplies such as chemicals, and a transportation network to deal with the distinctiveness of that industry.

And most of all, you need experienced personnel to maintain and run the equipment. The US has lost, and continues to lose, all of that to the Eastern Asian developing countries. They have bought our machinery, old as they are, and are doing the same thing my wool mill is doing - rebuilding and refitting the equipment. And they have also taken our infrastructure including our skilled labor.

Why is this taking place? It saves labor costs. But are we saving costs? Let's analyze this. My experience in building Wool Mill # 2 allows me to pass along some cogent remarks about this subject.

China will not permit a majority ownership by foreign companies, so our companies are "partnering" with their companies or are contracting with them by outsourcing production. China, the last time I looked at a map, is about half way on the other side of the globe, a great distance from the US market. Distance means transportation, which means costs and delays. In the textile world, delays are extra costly due to style changes and the fickleness of the ever-changing consumer desires.

Let's remember that China is an atheistic, communist government-run country with all the perils that go with the philosophy of socialism. It could confiscate our investments at anytime. Being a nuclear power, it is investing huge sums of the money it is getting from us into its military due to the enormous trade imbalance with us.

Take a look at the Los Angeles/Long Beach Seaport, the largest seaport in volume of imports and exports in the US. Look at the huge number of rusting steel cargo containers. This is because there is little trade in merchandise going from the US to China. It is too expensive to use a freighter to transport empty containers back to China.

Observe the quality of manufacturing or better stated, the poor quality and even the dangerous merchandise coming from that country. There is little American on-site quality supervision going on, resulting in the recalls that are in progress.

I have an economic theory that goes this way. The price of all resources including labor, such as water, seeks its own level. For example: labor costs are much higher in the US than in China. This is a given. Labor costs are greater and the number of laborers employed in China is rising. At some time, the labor differential will disappear. Because of the large number of impoverished workers in China, this will take longer to accomplish.

I remember reading that during World War II the Japanese labor force was getting two cents per hour. Our companies set up plants to take advantage of the labor cost differential. According to *World Trade 100* magazine, today's labor force in Japan "…is paid higher hourly labor costs than their counterparts in the US or the European Union…"

So where was I going to get skilled help for my second wool mill? The people we hired to help us get the mill going didn't care about quality, weren't interested in relocating to Virginia, were too expensive, took advantage of our temporary lack of experience, and would up and quit without notice. We were lacking experienced labor. What to do? Diane and I convinced our son, Scott, to learn to operate and maintain the equipment and so with our production manager, Joann's husband, Jerry, whose love of cars turned him into a skilled mechanic, we learned about the innards of the wool card.

I remember the first day's undertakings. Scott told Jerry, "How are we going to ever figure out this machine? I have seen it operating many times, but…"

Jerry said, "I look at the fifty-nine foot monster and I see gears, clutches and belts, just like cars."

"But look at the size of this thing. How will we ever figure it out? It takes years to train a person," Scott added.

"Your dad and this company haven't years to get this going. We will look at the section where the machine starts and forget, for the time being, the rest of the machine," said Jerry. "We will concentrate on one section at a time and learn all about it step by step."

And so the process began of cultivating our own employees to become skilled in the wool business. Day by day, Jerry and Scott mastered the workings of the giant wool card. We also brought in Ray, a retired electrician and a man of many mechanical talents. Little by little, error by trial error, things started to come together. When they mastered one thing, another problem arose. It was like two steps forward, one step back. But as I told them, "We are further ahead by one step each time."

They mastered lesson after lesson and finally quality production was underway. We hired a man with forty-four years experience in card maintenance and operations to visit us at some high cost and show us the finer points. During his three-day consultation, we learned more in an hour than we did in months from all the prior supposed experts combined.

I am so proud of Scott and the folks who helped him. The quality of yarn coming out of our mill is some of the best I have ever seen. We have completed the second wool card that will double our production volume. Skilled help is now in place and we will train future operators and keep the infrastructure in house.

The Environmental Protection Agency has approved our dyes to be safe for man, animals, fish and birds. Consent has come through from zoning for a dye house. There are hardly any left in this country. Once in place, we will save money on transporting fiber to and from a dye house and further improve the quality of work. We also have Joanne, a master dyer whose artfulness in designing and producing colors is a blessing.

Chapter 30

Shepherds' Remedies

Shepherds have traditionally pastured their sheep in remote areas of the world. Even in our modern society, sheep are grazed in areas unsuitable for crops. Because of this, shepherds have had to devise methods to accomplish and rectify problems that they encountered because medical facilities are generally quite a distance from the sheep.

I want to pass on some of the remedies that I've learned as a shepherd, both from experience and knowledge that was passed down to me from my ancestors.

My earliest recollection is from when I was about eight or nine years old. One summer day, my dad, Grandfather Cestari, and I were eating lunch near a wooded area on Long Island when I decided to take off into the woods. "Be careful!" my father said.

"You don't know what you're going to run into," said Grandpa.

Wearing only shorts, and no shirt, shoes or socks, I was "nature boy" personified from the 1940s Nat King Cole song. After running a short distance, my bare feet stomped into something that felt like some fallen leaves and small sticks. A nest of the yellow jackets was all but destroyed and its inhabitants were not happy to have my foot invade their home. Dozens of the wasps zeroed in and viciously attacked me, stinging me on every part of my exposed body.

I began running back to my father and grandfather. The pain was increasing as the wasps followed and didn't let up from their stinging and biting. Crying and panicked, I finally reached my dad and grandfather. They sized up the situation immediately and took charge as we were far from any medical facility.

The two grabbed me, laid me down on the ground and my grandfather took his knife and cut an x on each sting and pulled out a stinger. Afterwards, when we all calmed down, he instructed me to urinate in a cup. He then poured the urine on all of the stings. I was apprehensive about that remedy, but followed his instructions.

"You'll be fine," my grandfather assured me. The warm urine brought immediate soothing relief. Within an hour, it was as though nothing had happened. The welts receded and the pain dissipated.

More recently I had a problem with athlete's foot. For more than a year, with itching and burning between my toes, I tried every possible over-the-counter solution, all to no avail, even after seeing a podiatrist. So I decided to use my "atom bomb." I poured urine over the afflicted areas and within two days, I felt relief and the fungus disappeared.

Within our bodies we have remedies for many ailments. I believe that the uric acid, eliminated in urine along with other elements, dries up the sores and starts nature on its way to a cure. In an emergency when water is unavailable, drinking your own urine could save your life. It's an amazing byproduct of the human body.

Speaking of liquid, sheep are unbelievable at finding sources of water and will lead the shepherd to them. If any water is around, they will find it. The winter of 2010 is the worst in my memory having dumped at least eighty-four inches of snow in this part of the country. Sheep need water, so Diane and I discovered that they would literally dig a hole through the snow to get at a stream of water. Sheep are not stupid. Don't believe the cowboys who call sheep "dumb." However, sheep are stubborn.

Another shepherds' remedy is lanolin, which is natural oil from the sheep. It can work miracles on one's skin. This thick oil is used for many things such as a lubricant for machinery, musical instruments, and even cosmetics. Shepherds and wool-mill workers have wonderful skin because they handle lanolin all the time. In addition, it seems to delay signs of aging.

I've also discovered a solution to control ear wax buildup. I use alcohol and vinegar in a fifty-fifty mixture, and apply two drops into each ear canal. When I was a teenager, I developed severe acne. Thank God it didn't cause much scarring, as it was concentrated on my neck and back. I eventually grew out of it, and now, with my natural oils and exposure to lanolin, I seem to be avoiding wrinkles - at least up to now at age seventy-five.

Chapter 31

Government Subsidies

In the early eighties during Ronald Reagan's administration, I was operating my wool mill and doing some practicing of law and raising sheep. One day I received a phone call from a person who said that I was needed within the hour at the White House in Washington, DC. At first I was incredulous of the call but it was genuine. Mr. Armstrong was in charge of securing personnel to fill upper echelon positions in the federal government.

After realizing the authenticity of the call, I advised the caller that I needed more time as I was at least two-and-a-half-hours from Washington. Given the OK, I was asked for full particulars about the car I would be driving and all of my personal information so that the security guard would allow me on to the White House grounds. I still had no idea why I was being summoned.

Three hours later I arrived at the White House and was greeted by Mr. Armstrong. He took me into his spacious, beautifully appointed office located in the White House.

"Mr. Chester, do you know why you've been called here?" he asked.

"No, I don't."

"The president is considering appointing you to be the assistant secretary of agriculture for economic affairs," he said.

My jaw dropped, and to say the least, I was floored. I never gave much thought of working in Washington, DC. "Would you consider taking it?" Mr. Armstrong asked.

"Well, yes. I would." I said without another thought of how this would all play out with my family, law practice and farm. "What would be my area of responsibility?"

"President Reagan wants to eliminate farm subsidies and would like someone with your credentials to travel the country and convince farmers and ranchers of the negative aspects of farm subsidies," he explained. This was right down my proverbial alley. There were many, many more questions over the next several hours.

When the questions stopped, Mr. Armstrong stood up and told me that he was going to advise Secretary of Agriculture John Block that he found the perfect man for the job. I asked him what specific qualifications I had that he felt would be important to the post. He indicated my being an attorney, economics professor, and sheep man - a great combination for the position.

"If you are nominated, the selection will have to be approved by the US Senate and a public hearing would most likely be convened."

When I left the White House, I called Diane and both of us were beside ourselves figuring how this came about. As I drove back through Washington traffic and headed to my farm, my thoughts were clear about my beliefs on the subject of all kinds of subsidies. If they don't directly benefit all in society, then they should be abolished. There are precious few that I would support. The ones I endorse certainly include vaccinations for poor children, the National Health Institute's grants to individuals and institutions for approved research, support for those who are truly disabled in mind or body and cannot help themselves, and similar sorts of programs.

Subsidies such as the ones given to farmers for not growing crops and other various handouts, and maritime subsidies are not good and are unnecessary. The true market forces, not oligopolies and monoplanes controlling the market, are the way to go.

It's just so unfair that people who work and pay taxes, companies that provide work and produce goods and services and pay taxes, should lot have their good, hard-earned tax money go towards supporting non-productive activities of government. It's unfair and unjust. It is legalized stealing. Government, at all levels, is just too big.

Government must be responsible for the common good doing things they do best, such as protecting our country from its enemies, building and maintaining an efficient infrastructure, research, preservation of our national and state parks and wilderness areas, police and fire protection, and keeping individuals and businesses honest. Activities that can be performed best by the market place need be left there. With that political philosophy, taxes can be greatly reduced.

It was several weeks before I heard from anyone regarding the assistant secretary of agriculture for economic affairs position. Finally, I received notification from Senator Jessie Helms of North Carolina and Senator John Warner of Virginia that the economics advisor to the US Senate was finally selected. I was advised that it was down to two choices, the one selected and myself. For what it's worth, it was an interesting time, and even though I wasn't selected, I am privileged to have been considered.

Chapter 32

Evil Thrives When Good Men Do Nothing — Lord Edmond Burke, M.P. England 1729-1797

Each of us has a God-given obligation to be a good example and to fight when we see things amiss. Many times it is not easy to stand up and be counted. It's so much easier to act like sheep and merge into the crowd and not be observed. In other words, it's easier not to make waves.

To be a shepherd in life and be a leader takes standing up and being counted and not being afraid. God made lots of sheep and few shepherds, but it takes only a few and, even at times, just one shepherd to turn the herd around and make a difference in life.

As an attorney, I seemed to have attracted many unusual and sometimes controversial cases. Every time I take on one, I immediately have a friend, my client, and depending on the number of defendants, a number of enemies in direct proportion to the number of defendants.

Take this case in point. There was an elderly couple, in their upper eighties as I recall, who lived alone in a large, old mansion built in pre-Civil War time. It was located on the residue of a once large farm. A pipeline that ran through several different properties to the top of a small mountain artisan spring supplied the water to their home and livestock barn. The spring was protected by what is known as a spring house and was very well maintained.

One day a very wealthy man bought the farm that contained the springhouse that supplied all of the elderly couple's water requirements, as it had for over one-hundred-fifty years without interference by any of the neighbors, The law recognizes that if you use real estate long enough you can get what is known as a prescript easement on the property, in Virginia, such use must occur for twenty continuous years. If you lay claim to ownership and occupy it with intent that you own it (fifteen years in Virginia) then you could acquire title by adverse possession.

This waterline was a deeded easement. The wealthy man decided that he did not want an easement on his property, knowing however, that when he bought the property this waterline lawfully existed. Regardless, he proceeded to lay damage to it, curtailing this elderly couple's water.

I agreed to represent them and in so doing I made twelve enemies of defendants who owned the various properties that the water line crossed. They too wanted to terminate the easement. When I walked into court. these twelve people gave me looks that could have launched the Queen Mary. We won the case to the disdain of these twelve people.

The wealthy landowner called me afterwards and asked me if I could persuade my clients to terminate the easement and he would pay to install county water. He just didn't get it; my clients loved that fresh, clear, bubbling water from that spring.

I have had cases in which I defended clients and the press declared them guilty by "trial of the press." Subsequently, after a lawful trial, My clients were declared innocent. Lawyers, if they are true to themselves, make friends and also enemies. There is an old saying: *If you die without making an enemy, then you have done nothing in life.*

Chapter 33

The Death Penalty

Society has done much soul searching about the issue of whether punishment for crimes should include the death penalty. Many countries and some states have either had it abolished or have severely restricted its use.

Tradition has always held that a state has the right to protect itself from dangerous forces and people. In Christian theology this is reinforced by the biblical description of Jesus being interrogated by Pilate who asked him, "Where are you from?" Jesus did not answer him. So Pilate said, "Do you not speak to me? Do you not know that I have power to release you and I have power to crucify you?"

John 19:9-11 states the answer Jesus gave: "You would have not power over me if it had not been given to you from above." So there is no question, theologically, that a state has the God-given power to execute those deemed dangerous to society. The current argument against executions is that they are no longer needed to keep society safe because a person can be incarcerated for life, as prisons are impervious to escape.

But are they? I know of several instances in which dangerous inmates have broken out from what were considered escape-proof modern prisons. I live fewer than five miles from a modern prison. Not too long ago an inmate escaped from this prison by somehow getting into a trash truck and fleeing. It was reported that he then traveled to the railroad tracks that traverse our farm and hitched onto a freight car heading west. He was captured some forty miles away when he tried to get some food.

At this same prison, not long ago, two dangerous prisoners killed a third inmate by knifing him one hundred times with a handmade knife. In Texas, an inmate on death row escaped and while free, murdered a Texas Ranger who had a wife and two children.

Some thirty years ago before Louisa County had a public defender system in place to represent indigent defendants, I was asked by the circuit court to represent one of three defendants charged with the brutal rape of a young girl. It seems while traveling through Louisa County, these three individuals stopped at a moonshine maker to acquire some liquor. While there, they brutally gang raped the owner's daughter, almost leaving her for dead. She survived but what a lasting nightmare she must have.

In checking my client's criminal record I found that he had previously been convicted in New Jersey of murdering, on separate occasions, two of his relatives, and battering several others on separate occasions. Why was this individual out to commit more mayhem? The jury gave one of the other defendants, after finding him guilty, thirty days in prison. The judge was furious and gave my client and the other defendant thirty days saying that if society wants that, he will give them the same treatment. More mayhem to follow!

These are only a few of many examples of dangerous inmates escaping, or while in prison committing more murders. The problem I see with no death penalty is that when an individual has life in prison without parole, what potential punishment can be given to the person if they murder again – life in prison without chance of parole? He already has that sentence. There are no more deterrents for more serious crimes.

As long as there are people running the prisons, such things as pay offs, mistakes, carelessness, mechanical malfunctions and God-knows-what-other mismanagements, prisoners will escape and possibly becoming a mortal danger to society.

Just as there is no such thing as an unsinkable ship, there is no such thing as a prison from which an inmate can't escape. I agree that if such a prison system existed, and with society positively safe, there is no need for executions. Life being what it is, there is no possibility that society will ever be perfectly safe from dangerous criminals confined to prison.

What would the families of all the victims of prison escapees and killings inside of prisons say about the safety of our prisons? As I am writing this chapter and look out of my home library seeing the bucolic beauty of this farm, I am brought back to reality as I hear about the prison break involving an inmate who is serving a forty-five-year sentence for serious crimes. Somehow he managed an escape into a large wooded area near Richmond. Apparently after escaping, he broke into a home and acquired some weapons. Fortunately, the son of the property owner managed to fight off the escapee and confiscated the weapons from him and the inmate continued his run into the woods.

The department of corrections has dispatched more than four hundred correctional officers to the scene, and they have been searching for this convict with bloodhounds and vehicles for more than forty-eight hours without success. This will cost the state at least three-hundred to five-hundred thousand dollars depending on the length of time it takes to find the fugitive. Our state's prisons are understaffed because most people do not like to work there. With understaffed prisons, what would happen if there is another similar incident?

Where will the state get help? I suppose they would ask the National Guard, but it is also understaffed with problems overseas and the natural disasters currently plaguing our country. Escape-proof prisons? Don't believe it.

Chapter 34

My Bitch with the Legal System

After practicing law for more than fifty years, my view of the route law has taken since I began my journey is varied.

In 1961, when I closed on an all-cash real estate matter, all that was needed was: a title report, making sure the seller had good title to the subject property, a deed, and a cash-in and cash-out statement on my stationery. If a buyer was taking out a mortgage, add a note and mortgage to the above. Today, a closing involves a one-and-a-half, to two-inch pile of documents, one of which is an affidavit that the buyer is who he says he is after providing numerous documents of proof. What numbskull came out with this one!

Today, in law suits, there is a procedure known as discovery. Representing attorneys, if they choose to, may send opposing counsel a request for interrogatories and a demand for documents. My humble opinion is that this system has little benefit to the clients. How can anyone read packages of responses weighing pounds, and, in some cases, stacked papers measuring one foot high? It's great for the bottom-line attorneys, but not anyone else. To begin with, how does anyone know the truth of the documents?

Years ago we researched cases via an investigator, or an attorney did the leg work. The truth was then known to the client at a lower cost, whereas now it takes more time to read and investigate the truth of the documents. It's actually double work.

My definition of a brief is a document about a case explained by using few words, concise and succinct in a written argument that is submitted to a court. I have seen briefs written by attorneys that look like small to medium-sized books. Somehow they must feel that the more they write, the more they can charge a person.

A brief is as follows:

A concise statement of facts

Question or questions presented

Applicable law, both statutes stated and case previously presented, and finally, Argument of one's position.

After a few pages you are wasting your time and the judge's. I truly believe that a judge, and anyone for that matter, would be more inclined to read intently a short presentation rather than an enlarged brief.

In Virginia I took on an adoption case for a woman who had sexual relations with several men within the time frame of her fertile period. She conceived and had a child. She gave the child up for adoption to her sister and brother-in-law soon after giving birth. The adopting parents came to me to process the legal papers. The mother executed the necessary release but she could not identify the potential father or his whereabouts. For two years I tried to get the adoption completed, but the judges turned it down because the name of the child's father was unknown. A pregnant woman driving along could decide to have an abortion and, without any consent from the father, do so. Two hours later the woman, minus her now-dead child, is on her way back home. Is this justice? Does this make sense? No, and no.

We are burying ourselves in senseless rules and laws. Our legislature in Virginia this year submitted just under three-thousand bills for consideration as laws to be completed in less than ninety days. How can one-hundred-forty individuals have enough time to give serious consideration to that maw law proposals? They can't, and the result is stupid laws on the books.

The legal profession has to deal with federal laws, administrative rules that act as laws, federal court rules, local court rules, court decisions, and the US Constitution – and that's just within our federal system. Then there are each state's laws, rules, local rules and the state's constitution, plus administrative rules that act as laws. Moreover, there are the county, city and town's laws and rules and administrative rulings that also act as laws. We have turned our legal system into a monster.

Here is my suggestion: Give congress and each state legislature one year to do nothing but review all the administrative agencies' rules, all the laws on the books, and pass only laws eliminating useless, burdensome rules and laws, or no new laws or rules for that year.

Next, I submit my suggestions for our confounded tax structure. On the federal level, eliminate every single tax on the books, eliminate the Internal Revenue Service and have one national sales tax to run the federal government. Eliminate all subsidies including, but not limited to, ones for farm, Merchant Marine, and others such as public radio, bio fuel, and solar and wind power.

I do not take any subsidies from the government for my farm or for anything else. For two years, I received the wool subsidy and one year I had a credit for retaining ewes because I believed I was helping the sheep industry. That was pure nonsense, and I've not done it again. Although subsidies can help a few, I have not seen one example that proved they helped the country.

Lawyers need to get back to the basics of practicing law and act as proponents for the people.

> *Woe to you lawyers also. For you load men with burdens*
> *hard to bear, and you yourselves do not touch the burdens*
> *with one of your fingers. - Luke 12:46*

Jesus also told that Pharisees that "laws are made for man, not man for the laws."

What is being said here is that good laws enunciated by man are from God and are to be made to aid and benefit, and not to be burdensome and make it difficult for man to survive. Most of the laws and rules today are burdensome causing more havoc than is needed.

A bookkeeper comes to my office every Friday mainly to pay taxes and fill out forms for the government. This is so unnecessary since we are taking away from productive time to comply with nonsensical rules and regulations. Our God-given freedoms are being eroded.

The symbol of God is a circle and is the most simplistic symbol in nature. No beginning and no end. It is interesting that the circle is the basis for the well-known smiley face. This symbolizes itself to me as God being the source of joy and happiness.

The bottom line is that we must return to more simple ways or we will perish from these legalistic norms. Law is from God and is beautiful when beneficial. Lawyers must be protectors of them and not only for their sole monetary benefit, but also to help create a society that is honorable and peaceful.

Chapter 35

Grandparents as Substitute Parents

A few years ago I had a set of grandparents who asked me to represent them against their unmarried daughter who had two children by two different men, and neither father was supporting his respective child. The grandparents claimed that their daughter did not want them to visit with her children.

I filed a petition with the local juvenile and domestic relations court to have the case heard. Many states call this type of judiciary, the family court. Our juvenile and domestic relations court has somewhat limited jurisdiction as to what cases it can hold. I have long hoped that our state would bring about a family court where all matters such as adoption, custody, divorce, and crimes involving family members and the like could be heard. There is not such a system, so jurisdiction is somewhat divided, and at the same time concurrent, which makes it inefficient and costly to deal with such matters.

After investigating the case and interviewing witnesses, we proceeded with my clients' day in court. When the grandparents demonstrated that they had been very involved with the grandchildren, I was able to win visitation for them.

A short time later, in 2000, in the case of Troxel vs. Granvillle, the US Supreme Court said that if a parent does not want to extend visitation rights to the grandparents, then the parent has the right to do so. Bottom line: grandparents have no rights to compel visitation. Period.

The way around that is for grandparents to sue their daughter or son for a grandchild's custody on the grounds that their child, the mother or father, is not a good parent and is unable to raise the child properly. The grandparents must also establish that it would be in the best interest of the child for custody to be given to the grandparents. I have been very successful in doing this.

Many of the contemporary young generation with children have no real conception of what raising a child is all about and it is not entirely their fault. People born in the fifties and earlier were reared with stricter upbringing than today. A phrase most common back then was: *A child is to be seen and not heard.* What this meant was that parents came first. Today we see signs saying "children first." In my opinion this basic philosophy is all wrong. Society is putting children on a pedestal and they have become spoiled, lazy, and lack respect for their elders. Children seem to expect to get paid for everything that they do in the family.

A family should work together and pool its funds for the household's common good. That's what the Cestari family and my grandparents did and wealth ensued. Children had chores to do and they best did them. You wouldn't then hear the plaintiff of today whining, "I'm bored, there's nothing to do."

Our children were reared on our farm from the start and they knew responsibility early on. As Diane and I performed farm chores together as a family, she, or I would strap whoever was the infant on our back.

Children have disrespectful attitudes towards their elders because parents are permissive in raising their children and refuse to demand respect. Another common statement that I hear is: *I want better for my children than I had.* Foolish talk. Many children of today feel entitled believing the world owes them a living. Wrong. The world owes no one anything. "If a man will not work, he shall not eat..." is written by St. Paul in 2 Thessalonians 3:10 and reaffirmed by Captain John Smith at Jamestown when he told the starving settlers that "the greater part must be more industrious, or starve…" (Colonial Williamsburg Journal 1994).

To demonstrate some of my points, a single father came to me with a warrant against him for assault and battery brought by his seventeen year old "child". It seems that the father, my client, had been having serious discipline problems with his daughter. She was into sex and was going around with a no-count boyfriend who was apparently using his daughter. My client had warned his daughter to stay away from Mr. No-Count, but she refused.

After their confrontation, she left home for two days and stayed with Mr. No-Count. She finally returned at four a.m. on the third day. The father approached her and told her that she was grounded for thirty days - no car, the works. She gave him her usual disrespectful sass and went to bed. The next day she awoke at noon and headed for the car. My client went after her and demanded that she get out of the car. She refused. He forced her out of his car and when she became real ugly to him, he proceeded to place her over his lap and gave her a slap with his hand on her rear. She ran into her room and called the sheriff's department who came and arrested him and charged him with assault and battery, punishable by up to one year in jail and/or a twenty-five-hundred-dollar fine.

I told my client that he did the right thing to regain control over an obviously errant child.

The case was held before Judge Harrison May at the Augusta Juvenile and Domestic Relations District Court. After all the evidence was in, I addressed the court with my closing argument. "Judge, a parent has the right and the obligation to use reasonable force if necessary to bring a child into compliance. Spanking this child on her bottom was clearly reasonable force. If you find my client guilty then this will be something of a signal to the community that children can do whatever they want without consequences. While you're at it let's hand the key to the jail house inmates and let them out."

Judge May agreed and said, "Miss, your father had a perfect right to do what he did. The good Lord gave padding to the rear for just such occasions. Sometimes this is needed to relocate one's brains back to the head. Another thing, if you file charges ever again against your dad for a similar manner, I will have you put in jail". Case was dismissed.

That's the kind of ruling we need in support of parents and teachers. I am not advocating cruelty, but I do see a place for reasonable physical force to bring about order. We, as a society, must have order and one has to do what is reasonable to have that. There is no law that says you can't use reasonable restraints and physical force. It seems everybody is afraid of a lawsuit. Forget it. We, as a society, must rear our children to meet reasonable standards of respect and discipline. A wild horse is worth practically nothing until trained and disciplined. The same goes for children. A respectful and disciplined child is a loving and productive child.

Grandparents are becoming more involved in the raising of their grandchildren and I do not think this bodes well for our society. Let them make their mistakes and *allow* them to learn from them. I see it all the time. Of course I understand that there are times when grandparents need to interfere for the benefit of a grandchild. However, grandparents need to compel their wayward children to pay the consequences of their misdeeds – financially in maximum child support, and embarrassment to boot.

And then I had these grandparents come up against the following. Their daughter had a child out of wedlock without the father's support, and they wanted to help their daughter. Sometime later, this daughter had another child also out of wedlock with another man. I tried to tell the parents to stop helping their daughter as she was using them.

Their daughter had a third out-of-wedlock child. The daughter was having "fun" around town while her parents took care of the children. The grandparents finally woke up. I had a conversation with this girl to find out why she was throwing away her life.

"Men think I'm ugly, so very few men want me," she said.

This was ridiculous! She was a beautiful girl, but had low self esteem as do many of today's girls.

I have parents who are housing and boarding a daughter or son with their live-in boy or girlfriend. This is paid in-full fornication. Their argument: At least we know where they are. This is giving their children the green light to do wrong! What examples they are setting for their children.

On the subject of cohabitation, not only is it and has been immoral for millennia, but it also doesn't work. Government statistics show that those who engage in sexual relations without benefit of marriage have a ninety-five percent chance of breaking up. Of the five percent remaining, they marry and half of them get divorced. That's a two and a half percent chance of success. Would you go to a gambling house and bet with a chance of ninety-seven-and-a-half percent chance of losing? That's only money. These low morals and life-setting patterns have serious consequences, and I believe the reason is lack of trust in each other.

I think women are the greatest gift that God gave to the world. Every one is a creation of beauty. If there were only men in the world, this place would self-destruct. Women bring class to the world; women bring culture to the world; women bring morality to the world.

Women of the world do what's right and force change in this sick society.

Chapter 36

Mental Illness

Mental illnesses are plaguing our society as never recorded before. Years ago the unfortunate people suffering with mental problems were warehoused in institutions called insane asylums. They were just that – warehouses for humanity. Society knew no cures for mental illnesses and so the mentally ill would end up in these buildings.

In the twentieth century, society started looking into how the brain functions, and little by little causes and cures were discovered. Sigmund Freud, who died in 1939, contributed much to the science of mental illness. He was the catalyst who drew attention to ailments of the brain and got science to devote research into the mysteries of the mind.

Psychiatry and psychology are relatively new sciences. The study of mental illnesses is still in its infancy, and there is so much that must be done and can be accomplished with the proper research.

During my fifty years of practicing law, I have seen many clients suffering with mental illnesses. Now, I see more of it than ever. Eight percent of the general population is suffering from ADHD, or Attention Deficit Hyperactivity Disorder. However, eighty percent of the prison population suffers from this affliction with many others experiencing other forms of mental illnesses such as bipolar disorder. Does that mean that all who endure these disorders wind up going to prison? No, but It certainly can lead to that.

Here's another statistic. Over eighty percent of the prison population – in the United States, 2.2 million – is there due to some form of alcohol and/or drug addiction. If we could remedy the causes of people running to these addictions, wonders could be accomplished. Much of mental illness is brought about by inherited maladjusted genes and environmental factors such as brain injuries.

Science now knows that there is a gene that runs in certain families that contributes to alcoholism. While attending college, I knew some Irish men there. A number of them, and their ancestors, had taken an oath of abstention from alcohol. They vowed to God that they wouldn't go near alcoholic beverages because they had a family tree of alcoholism Yes, alcoholism can be an inherited problem. It is the same with drugs. It takes a strong-willed person knowing this to abstain, and what a better person he or she is who acknowledges this and takes the necessary steps to avoid these substances. We need to offer better support to these people.

Also in college, I had a friend who drank to extreme. Eugene was one of the most brilliant individuals I ever knew, and a fine individual when not drinking. I would plead with him to stop. Once at a dance, he became so drunk that I found him in an awful state of vomiting. I held his head and asked him, "Why do you do this to yourself?" His response was, "It's great going down." Here was an individual who won a full scholarship to college and found learning a joke because it was so easy to him.

Ten years after graduation, he died of alcoholic poisoning leaving two young children and a wonderful wife. What a wasted life. He could have accomplished so much for himself, his family, and society. I often think of Eugene. At graduation from college in 1957 we had seven, yes seven seniors who died in automobile crashes because they were drunk. What a waste of education and human life.

Each year thirty thousand people commit suicide due mostly to mental illnesses. Many innocent victims are among them. Twenty-five thousand people are killed in auto accidents due to substance abuse. If we lost that many people in battle in a year, we would be up in arms. But there's nary a whimper for these preventable deaths.

One day two parents came to me and presented the following set of tacts. The father had a missing leg and a non-functioning arm. It seems that one day he was driving his car when a drunk driver hit him head on almost killing him. That's how he lost his limb and use of an arm. He never drank alcoholic beverages in his life. His wife, sitting next to him in my office, admitted that she was a recovering alcoholic.

They had a son who seriously abused alcohol. He was a mean drunk and they said that one night he came to their home as drunk as can be. For no apparent reason, he went into his parents' room and started beating his poor father with his own cane. They called the sheriff's office and their son was taken in, but he was later returned to his parents' home.

This couple came to me and pleaded for me to get help for their son whom they still loved. The mother had found their son the night before stretched out drunk in the gutter, and she brought him home.

This young man was in a desperate state and needed help. His parents asked me to try to get him admitted to our local mental institution and I tried everything, going before several judges. Each one said it was not in their power to commit him. I finally was able to have him enrolled in a seven-day alcoholic program called New Hope. On the seventh day, New Hope called and said that they were going to release him that evening. I rushed to the recovery facility and my client pleaded with me to get him in the mental facility next door.

I brought in the director of the unit and told her that my client needed long-term help and asked that he be admitted next door. She turned to my client and told him, "You are going to be all right. Aren't you?"

He said, "If you release me I will get drunk and I will hurt somebody." She laughed and released him. True to his word, he did get drunk and someone did get hurt.

Another parent came to me needing help for her daughter who was in her late twenties. She had four children from several fathers, and had already spent a majority of her adult life in prison for various forms of theft. This time, she was facing a long sentence for twelve counts of illegal use of credit cards. It seems that while cleaning a police chief's office, she stole one of his credit cards and made purchases until caught.

The first thing I did was get her a psychological evaluation. Why was she repeating thefts knowing full well, as before, she would get caught. She was diagnosed with a serious mental illness and had not previously had any psychological help. She had been warehoused in prison, never getting the help she desperately needed. Her psychological tests indicated that if she wasn't put on prescribed drugs, she would continue to commit thefts.

When I was a young boy, my dad and I would routinely go by a major mental facility where several thousand patients were institutionalized. They had a huge farm and many patients worked the farm. We didn't have anywhere the number of mass killings and injuries by mentally ill people because they were institutionalized and cared for. Then in the 1960s, due to a class action suit, most of the patients were released and integrated into the general population. Many of these unfortunate people were being helped with discoveries in pharmacological assists. They were supervised in taking their prescribed drugs, and then turned out without supervision to ensure they continued taking their prescriptions. Why? They didn't like the fact that the drugs leveled out their ups and downs and they wanted to be in an excited stage which brought about trouble. Many discovered self-medicated "theories" along with alcohol and drugs, which made their anxiety worse.

Solutions: Legalizing illegal drugs is not the answer. That would only give society the imprimatur that these drugs are good for you. What we need to do is reopen and modernize our mental institutions and flow funds into employing qualified and dedicated mental health professionals, ones who will work with these people on an individual basis and ultimately get them qualified to rejoin the general population. They could gradually work with them and help them become useful citizens. There will be many who may not be able to live in society and they should be humanely cared for.

We have switched warehousing from mental insane asylums to prisons. Society needs to address mental illnesses in long-term settings and cut back on warehousing prisoners under the present turnstile system, in, out, back in.

Churches can certainly become more involved by increased pastoring and guiding these people about moral law, and helping them to see that they need to avoid persons, places and things that would lead them to do destructive things.

Also, mental patients should be helped to know how to look forward to each day. Give them educational trade and work programs. Let them realize that although they are sick, they are important to society. Give them hope. We need to think constructively, not destructively when it comes to criminal activities. Yes, there will always be incorrigibles who need to be in prison.

I am certainly not advocating that people who commit crimes should not have consequences to pay for their bad actions. Not at all, but punishment with a program of restoring criminals to society in a helpful manner could change things for the better.

Those who are incarcerated in prison should be given opportunities to be of service to society. Warehousing is a waste of time and money. Every human being needs to know that he or she is valuable, even convicts.

Chapter 37

Apologia

A formal defense and justification
for the Catholic Church

Almost every Tuesday, since I was well on the way toward finishing this book, I would meet with my editor who would query me and suggest points concerning this book. During one meeting, she asked, 'If you had your way, I think you would want everyone who reads your book to be a Catholic. Is that so?"

Without hesitation, I answered, "Yes."

I did some soul searching about that question and response.

Why the question? And why such a positive response?

After much thought, I developed this chapter. I wanted to defend, and explain my faith.

The Catholic Church for almost fifteen hundred years was the only Christian religion in the world. It existed as the one and only expression of the Christian tradition.

Jesus, the Messiah, established one church of faith believers. Prophesy had it that the messiah would come from the Jewish tradition and so he did, but he was not what many of the Jews expected. They were looking for a messiah who would be a political figure, and one who would restore the Jews to be free people independent of foreign rule. And so Jesus was rejected as their messiah and faithful Jews still wait for their messiah.

From the beginning, Christ opened his church to Jews and to Gentiles. The church has been attacked and persecuted down through the ages by Christians and non-believers, but the church has withstood outside attacks.

In 1517 at a University at Wittenberg, Germany, a Catholic monk named Martin Luther posted ninety-five theses of objections he found concerning the Catholic Church. Some of these dealt with indulgences, which absolved one for full or partial temporal punishment for sins, and during the Middle Ages were granted in exchange for donations to the church. They were admittedly improperly promoted and there were unfortunately inappropriate things going on that needed correction.

Here, allow me to point out the following Christian beliefs. God is perfect, Jesus is God, and the Catholic Church (originally called Christian

Church) was founded by Jesus. He placed the church in the hands of imperfect people who are subject to sin. Therefore, activities of people in the church could result in problems.

And here is the point. For fifteen hundred years, the church had seven sacraments: baptism, the Eucharist (Holy Communion), confirmation, penance, holy orders, matrimony, and the sacrament of the healing (formerly known as extreme unction).

Martin Luther said that only one qualified as a sacrament instituted by Christ: baptism. Catholics believe in transubstantiation, with the words by a duly ordained priest, the bread and wine are truly the body and blood of Christ. It is the unbloody sacrifice of the cross although the physical properties of bread and wine are unchanged. Luther rejected the concept of transubstantiation and thus, Holy Communion as a sacrament.

Luther abolished extreme unction, denied penance and accepted confirmation, matrimony and ordination (holy orders) as rites, but not sacraments. So for fifteen-hundred years, the words of one person are no longer. The Catholic and Orthodox Church are the only Christian churches that go back directly to the apostles. If the apostles administered seven sacraments and all of the early church fathers administered seven sacraments, do we abolish six out of the seven because a few in the church, at that time, had problems with them?

I contend that Catholics, at the time, recognized manmade errors and set about correcting them via the Council of Trent during the years 1545-1563. Because of ecclesiastic, political and on-going wars the Council didn't occur as soon after Martin Luther's denunciations. If it had occurred sooner, possibly the damage could have avoided splitting the Christian church into fractions.

My point is that Catholics acknowledged that the baby (church) was dirty and needed cleansing. They washed the baby and restored the church and its traditions and abolished errors. Protestants tossed the baby and the dirt out together thus creating a whole new manmade church.

One of the saddest lessons that I learned from my former secretary, Roslyn, was concerning the Holocaust. It seemed that her grandparents and close relatives were all victims of that disaster. She shared with me much about her Jewish faith and the historical fight for survival. I have had and continue to have great admiration and caring for the Jews.

Let us not forget that Jesus, his mother, foster father, and the first Christians were Jews and the first half of our Bible is based on that of the Jews. Great people.

Chapter 38

Personal Experiences with the Sacraments

The Catholic Church instructs that the seven sacraments are essential for believers. Although not everyone must receive all sacraments, they are necessary for salvation. The Church teaches that Christ imparts the grace of each sacrament, from forgiveness of sins to dedication of a particular service.

At this point allow me to share with you my personal experiences with the sacraments. Because my parents were having difficulties conceiving a child at the beginning of their marriage, my birth was a very special event in their lives. I was conceived in my mother's womb in 1935 and born January 25, 1936.

The times were difficult. The bank in which my dad and uncle kept their money closed its doors and they lost a substantial amount of money. My dad left the business. It wasn't until years later, when they received two percent on the dollar.

My mom and dad were working seven days a week to keep things together. Unemployment reached twenty-five percent with many people working only part time. It is a wonder that there were any children born at that time considering the conditions. The birth rate dropped to one of its lowest points in the history of the country.

Just weeks after I was born my parents had me baptized at St. Ritas Catholic Church. And with that, a spiritual bonding took place as a result of the administering of that sacrament. The bonding occurred amongst my parents, my godparents (Aunt Elma and Uncle Val), and me.

For a child's godparents, especially with Italians, the bond is both spiritual and traditional as they take on an important role in raising that child. The series of motion pictures entitled The Godfather, should've included "and the Godmother." She is a major influence, and behind every godfather is a godmother.

There was a large celebration held the day of my baptism, including a special white outfit for me representing original sin being washed away from my soul, and that my life was really beginning on that occasion.

When I was eight years old, the age of reason, my godmother and parents, with the help of nuns, prepared me to receive the sacrament of penance and Holy Communion. For penance, I was told to recall any actions or thoughts that were against the Ten Commandments. I was to know those commandments by heart and in order. My introduction to my first confession was initially a little scary. I had to go into a darkened booth in the church and kneel before a screen. Behind the screen sat a priest to whom I would begin talking with the words, "Bless me Father, for I have sinned. This is my first confession." I remember the kindness of the priest who helped me through this novel experience in my early life. I walked out with a feeling of relief and satisfaction that my sins were forgiven by God, armed with the suggestions by the good priest of how to improve my life. I could almost feel the graces upon me with the experience.

Then came the day I would receive the Lord in Holy Communion. My mother and dad bought me a dark blue suit to wear. Boys had a white ribbon on their sleeve, and girls wore beautiful white dresses, veils, and stockings. I can still see everyone in line to the altar. Afterwards, there was another traditional Italian festival!

Anytime the bishop came to our church was a special occasion. When I was twelve years old, I received the sacrament of Confirmation administered by our bishop. I was to choose a sponsor and also a name of a saint to whom I felt close. Strengthening our spiritual bond, I selected one of Aunt Elma's brothers as my sponsor. I chose (at my mother's strong suggestion) Henry as my middle name, a variation of Enrico, her father's name.

During the ceremony, the bishop asked each candidate, Do you want to be confirmed and become a soldier in Christ's army?" With my assent I became a defender of the faith, or a "soldier of Christ," anointed with oils, and slapped gently on my cheek as a reminder to be brave. Following that was yet another lively Italian festival with gifts and as always delicious Italian food.

I was honored to serve as an altar boy as an older cousin celebrated his first mass after receiving the sacrament of holy orders in which he became a Catholic priest. Father Bruno was a good and faithful priest whose last parish, before his death, was that of Saint Frances Cabrini in Brooklyn.

Matrimony, what a special sacrament. My own marriage to Diane was a wonderful experience. Married at St. John's Catholic Church in Chester, Vermont, in 1966, we had a nuptial mass, which gave us special blessings. Diane, although not a Catholic has kept her promise to raise our children in the Catholic faith. She has been an excellent counter balance in my life, helping me avoid some of its pitfalls.

And, finally I will write about the sacrament of healing, or the anointing of the sick. When a Catholic is dying, a priest is called to assist the individual by hearing his or her confession and giving Holy Communion if conscious. Holy oil is used to anoint and strengthen a person and reaffirm his or her confidence in God's power and good will. It is a beautiful procedure that I wish all people could experience.

The Church is there from the beginning of life, through life, and is there when one of its members is departing from this life. I have enjoyed, thus far, my journey through life with the Church as it is there and continues to be with me throughout.

Chapter 39

In Defense of God

God has had many appellations through the years. To list a few, He has also been called: *Deity, Allah, Supreme Being, I Am That Am, I Am Who Am, Yahweh, Jehovah* (a misreading of Yahweh), and *Adonis* meaning Lord, Lord, and Prime Mover.

God is defined as a person who had no beginning and will have no end: I am That Am; I Am Who Am. He is the alpha and the omega, first and last, with no ending, and Creator of all things physical and spiritual. He created all from nothing, prime mover, supreme giver of law, and source of all love and understanding.

The Jews, when writing the name God, would pen that word in gold and would address God as Adonai, meaning my lord, all in reverence to him. God had a personal relationship with the Jews. They were the first to understand and appreciate that there is but one God. At times, the Jews would take God for granted and would do wrong all to their eventual detriment. God would forgive them and welcome them back once they saw the error of their ways and returned to God for help. He was always there when they needed him.

Christianity acknowledges that there are three distinct persons in God. God the Father is attributed with creation. God the Son, Jesus, is the redeemer of his people. And God the Holy Ghost, or Holy Spirit, breathes life into souls and gives inspiration. Three persons, but one God. It is the most compelling mystery for mankind, only acceptable on faith as with many other things we accept in life.

Known as the Trinity, the three persons are a mystery subject to faith and not provable from reasoning or science. The existence of God. however, is provable from reason and from science. Yes, there is solid proof in the existence of God.

One is the concept of prime mover. Simply put it states that someone had to get the ball rolling, or get things started. Also, everything comes from something - where did the something come from? Who caused the something, and where did the something come from? Who started and how did that first something begin? It had to come from nothing to start with. Who is able to take nothing and make something? We call that person God, the prime mover: *Am That Am, I Am Who Am, Allah, Deity, Yahweh, Lord, and Adonai, Supreme Being.*

In addition, just look at the intricacies of nature; nothing like it could have developed without a supreme mind. Consider that from out of nothing something appeared and functions with precision.

Repeated surveys report that more than ninety-five percent of our people express a belief in God, over ninety-five percent! That leaves less than five percent who are agnostic, or ones who call themselves atheist.

Agnostics assert that all sources of knowledge are unknown and limited to one's own experience. They don't deny his existence; they just claim that God is not provable. On the other hand, atheists reject the existence of a supreme being, period.

Some say that there is no such thing as an atheist, especially when in a foxhole and death is all around. Even the word atheist is very interesting. A means one or to; theist means God. So an atheist, in strict English interpretation means one God or to God.

By their renouncing of God they are at the same time acknowledging his existence. Why would they put up such a fight, using the word for-to-one-God if they don't think he exists? Would you spend your time arguing over something that you know doesn't exist? Why bother? It appears that agnostics and atheists are trying to prove to themselves and to others who will listen, the nonexistence of God, and they can't. Try proving a negative when the provable positive exists.

For millennia, Jews, Christians and all others of belief have daily expressed their faith and their love for God, who was an integral part of their existence. There was a beautiful communication between God and his people. During the Middle Ages especially, edifices to the glory of God such as churches, magnificent works of art, sculptures and music were created by man to the glory of God.

Diane and I visited Italy on a pilgrimage to Rome, and Assisi, the birth and conversion site of Saint Francis, whose heart burned with passion for God. We were absolutely astonished at the centuries' old structures for worshiping God, built by people who didn't do it for money alone, but for a passionate love for God, who was and still is in Italy a part of their very existence. The word God is mentioned frequently and unashamedly.

Where have we come to in the country where over ninety-five percent of the people say they believe in God? Why are we so timid with our faith in God? Why should we be? He is the finest person, our best friend ever, who is always there, if we acknowledge him. God does not and will not force us to come to him and love him. That's our free will, the most precious gift ever given to mankind. He wants us to come to him and love him voluntarily instead of in a meaningless forced-to-love method. Voluntary love is so much more meaningful and is so much more beautiful. And so we have free will.

In the last several decades we have systematically excluded God in the public square. We act as if we are ashamed to mention and express our love for him publicly. School and the public buildings are becoming void of any expression of God. This is terrible and we are seeing the consequences of our shame and discomfort with public expression of God.

There is a law of nature. Nature hates a vacuum. Eliminate God in the public square and in our homes, and guess who enters the vacuum? The answer is: the evil one who is also called Satan, the great deceiver, and the devil. And God's original name for him, Lucifer, Angel of Light, was believed to be the most intelligent of creatures.

When God, who symbolizes order, peace and love, is removed by statute, court decisions, or what not, it opens the gate to chaos, war, and hate. We have to change. We cannot exist without a thorough, loving communication with God, a two-way conversation. Right now in most cases, it's God on the line and we're not there. How can we expect his help? Remember free will, it has to come from us voluntarily.

It seems so clear that if we wake up and ask God to come in, we can enjoy this wonderful world of beauty. Initially, when people depart from each other they leave with the word *addio*. In French it is *adieu* and in Spanish *adios*. All three mean depart and go with God. What a wonderful expression of faith.

And now my humble suggestions:

Express your faith…we all, one-hundred percent of our people, really do have faith and show it.

In letters and in words, tell your department friends *addio*, *adieu* or *adios* or have a blessed day.

Say prayers of gratitude for your food in restaurants.

Visit your churches, synagogues, mosques, and talk to God.

Say prayers with your family.

Display symbols of faith in your home, cars, trucks, and place of employment.

Let God and especially the people you come into contact with know of your love for God.

Demand that our government puts an end to God's isolation in the public square.

And sign off with *addio*, *adieu*, *adios* or God go with you.

Chapter 40

Assessments in Augusta County

In Virginia as in other states, the tax structure or cities and counties is based upon real and personal valuations. To base the values on real estate, which provides the lion's share of the local taxes, a mass assessment process takes place where each parcel of land is supposed to be appraised and assigned a market value. With Augusta County, as in many other counties, the assessment is performed every four years.

Augusta County had its assessment completed for January 1, 2009. When the results were published, the county's real estate owners were angry, as assessments were increased for almost all parcels, and greatly increased in most cases, despite the fact that real estate values were plummeting.

When I saw this, I decided that it was time to put a halt to increased unjust local taxation when the community's economics were very poor. I decided to see if the public would respond to such an effort. I enlisted Kurt Michael and Lynn Mitchell, both astute politicians and Jason Bivou, who at the time was a member of the Augusta County Sheriff's Office. He would later be fired by the sheriff for his political involvement - a most unjust firing if there was ever one.

Later, I was helped by Michael Roman, a county property owner who donated two thousand dollars so we could secure the benefits of an independent legal research firm, and Ed and Georgia Long, two very capable assistants.

The assessments were published in January 2009 and in February, we held a "Town Meeting" in a local church that we rented. The turnout was remarkable with the social hall and church packed with more than six hundred people on the inside and dozens more outside waiting to get in.

Tracy Piles, a member of the Augusta County Board of Supervisors, a competent ally, and I gave two talks to the gathering. Tracy was the only supervisor who stood against the illegal assessments.

I prepared a petition which, with help from the capable people mentioned above, was widely distributed around a county of just under one thousand square miles. The response was amazing with signatures of ten thousand, six hundred county property owners. This proved to be the largest political effort ever undertaken in our county.

In March of that year, I went to County Executive Patrick Coffield and requested that a special hearing be held to address the concerns of the people. A date was set.

My information indicated that there would be a massive turnout for that hearing. I pleaded with the county officials to hold the hearing at a nearby high school to accommodate the anticipated crowd. I was told "no." Their reasoning was that the largest number of people attending a hearing was two hundred, and they could handle it at their government center.

The night of the special hearing drew more than one thousand people who packed the government center, with several hundred more wanting to be admitted. The county employed a fire marshal from Northern Virginia (as Augusta County does not have a fire marshal) to keep the number of attendees low. The marshal limited the number of people the facility could safely hold to below the lawful capacity. Politics at work.

The Sheriff's Office was called out and it stationed side armed deputies at the entrance to keep the crowd at bay, including my wife, who arrived late after tending to our livestock. When four people would leave, one or two would be permitted to enter, causing deep anger from the outside crowd. It's a wonder there wasn't a riot.

A number of speakers, including myself, and good friend Joel Salatin, charged the board of supervisors with violating our rights by allowing illegal assessments to be used as the basis for setting the taxes. I presented all the signed petitions, which authorized me to legally represent them as their attorney, on a pro-bono basis, to get the illegal assessments set aside.

The board, except for Tracy Piles, totally ignored the petitions which were tied up with strands made from our yarn.

I then prepared to institute suits against the county for relief. I tried to get assistance from other members of the bar. Not one attorney, in all of Virginia would lend me any help, not even for research assistance. In frustration, I said to an attorney friend, "If I took all the spinal material from all the attorneys around, I would be lucky to make one usable spine."

"You're probably right," he said.

I was legally alone. My daughter and paralegal, Sabrina, and I were placed in the terrible position of putting together legal documents that dealt with unprecedented legal matters. The tax volume in Virginia, as reinforced by a legal expert researcher who was hired by Michael Roman (as it turned out too late in the proceedings) said that it was the most disorganized, discombobulated law book she had ever encountered.

Against the advice of Sabrina, I started to file anyway. She said we needed more time to prepare, but the pressure by the media and the public to file was enormous.

At a preliminary to the hearing session, Judge Victor Ludwig, the circuit court judge for the county, hinted that the procedure I was using might be questionable. Here again, against the advice of Sabrina, and trusting in this judge's off-the-cuff opinion, I filed a non suit.

These efforts proved to be fruitless and I was verbally attacked by Judge Ludwig in a seventeen-page opinion, and was reprimanded and sanctioned with a two-thousand-dollar fine. The sanction was totally uncalled for and unprecedented. It was beyond memory in our area for an attorney to be sanctioned. Many years ago, another attorney was sanctioned with only a reprimand and that was overturned by the Virginia Supreme Court and so I stood alone, sanctioned.

At this point, I wanted to get an attorney to help me with the appeal on the sanctions. Again, not one from the bar would lend assistance except one from Charlottesville, Virginia, who wanted at least ten. thousand dollars.

With assets such as land, sheep, and my farm, I was out of cash for two reasons. First, it was costing me time and out-of-pocket expenses to carry out these proceedings. Second, I was losing clients. Some retrieved their files, giving their business to a non-committal bar, as they told me they were afraid of the judge. They said they thought he had a personal vendetta against me and would hold It against them for hiring me.

My practice literally came to a screeching halt. I had a strong feeling that if I could take my sanctions to the State Supreme Court, they would be set aside.

Let me say to anyone who thinks he or she can fight a law suit without resources to forget it. The legal system today is set up so that the chief requirement to win a case is money. Without cash you are "barking up the wrong tree." Resources are the name of the game and I was depleted of them and so I had to let my pending appeal expire and face the consequences. And they came fast.

The county attorney brought on a motion for show cause asking the court to hold me in contempt because I had yet to pay the sanction. I certainly wasn't going to sell any of my fine sheep, as it would have set back my breeding program for years. I went before Judge Ludwig and told him the truth.

"I do not have the cash, presently, to pay the sanction. I will pay it. I need time."

Meanwhile, with no money coming in from the law practice and the wool mill operating part time because it was out of season, I went to the Staunton Mall and signed a lease to operate a farm market at its entrance. It was a huge success and was the only money coming in.

At the contempt hearing, Judge Ludwig ruled that I was not in contempt and gave me the requested time to pay the fine. As I was leaving the court room, several people told me not to pay the sanction because the people would.

I took them at their word, and soon the checks started to arrive. There were ones for five. Ten, twenty and twenty-five dollars; one family sent me five-hundred dollars. As they came in, I paid off the sanction fine. Ed and Georgia checked with the county treasurer as my full payment was approaching the deadline, and took care of the remaining balance.

In the meantime, Michael Roman offered to pay a legal research firm to make a last-ditch effort to salvage the assessment proceedings. Between that firm and my office, we came up with section 58.1-3003, a Nineteenth Century law with no appellate precedent.

This law stated that if one percent of the registered voters signed a petition (which I prepared) demanding the commonwealth's attorney to sue the county for an illegal tax levy, then the commonwealth's attorney must file suit. Lee Ervin, Augusta County's commonwealth attorney, and I worked together to prepare the suit and we had a lot more than one percent of registered voters' signatures.

At the hearing, Judge Ludwig reserved decision. After several months, he again ruled against the people. If this decision had been appealed to the Virginia Supreme Court, I felt that true justice would have prevailed. It would be what is known as a case of first instance or impression. I feel comfortable that the justice would have been interested in hearing this unusual case. The attorney general refused to allow Lee the authority to file the appeal. Figure out that one.

You may wonder why I had Judge Ludwig hear these cases in the first place. I did make motions to have him recuse himself, and he denied my motions. He was, and is, the judge for Augusta County. It does give me some consolation that several attorneys and two judges I spoke with were shocked at his rulings. The fact is, it did happen, and consequences followed that made me even more determined to overcome them.

Currently, I'm working with local members of the community to support and am actively campaigning for a new slate of candidates that will enable us to replace the existing government officials.

Initially, I put the Churchville farm up for sale and was determined to save the wool mill. So I made major changes in our wool mill marketing plans. First, we reduced the price of the three collections to one of the lowest in the hand-knitting yarn industry. It was our lowest price in thirty-five years. By reducing expenses and being careful to avoid duplications, we have been able to maintain quality at lower costs, and it is working. Sales are up and there is a new sense of enthusiasm with our customers. We are out to improve things all around.

The law office started to improve with clients rethinking their reluctance to patronize my office. The word is out that I wasn't destroyed by what happened and they may have recalled the many victories in the courtroom of past years, and figured there was still fight in this seventy-five-year-old man.

Our farm is opening a total of four farm market stands throughout Virginia's central Shenandoah Valley area this summer. The "For Sale" sign has been removed from the farm's silo and has been replaced with a huge sign that reads, "Nothing is Impossible with God" and He has proven that many times to me.

Good does come out of tough times. Sabrina, seeing that the law office was initially suffering, decided to apply to Ave Maria Law School in Naples, Florida, and was awarded a full St. Thomas Moore scholarship.

Chapter 41

Our Four Children

*"It is no use to preach to [children] if you do not act decently yourself." —
Theodore Roosevelt*

When Diane and I were first married, we decided to leave to God what children
we would have and we ended up with a total of four: three girls, and a boy, but it
was complicated! When I was sixteen years old, I contracted mumps and was
told that it had affected the mobility of my sperm. The doctor also said it was
improbable that we would be able to conceive any children, but God decided
otherwise! Of the four, we adopted two from Catholic Charities in Richmond,
Virginia, and two came naturally. The doctor said that the two biological children
were miracles. He was wrong! All four were miracles.

If you ask Diane or me who are the adopted children and who are our
biological children, we have reached the point that we have erased from our
minds any such distinctions. Each one of the four is our child; only their paths of
delivery to our home were different.

The four children are: Francis Scott, Angelique Gabrielle (named for the
Angel Gabriel), Jennifer Suzanne, and Sabrina Noelle.

Francis Scott (answers to Scott) is a fine young man who attended and
completed instruction at a police academy and worked in the local prison until it
was closed. He then asked Diane if she thought I would hire him for the farm, as
he had previously worked there part time. "I think your working with him would
make your father very happy," she told Scott.

I was so excited to know that my son elected to be a part of the
business full time. Scott has exceeded all my expectations as a son. He is loyal,
works hard, and although quiet and unassuming, takes command of things. A
perfectionist, Scott not only expertly performs his farm duties, including repairs
of equipment and laying cement blocks as needed, but he is also our chief wool
card operator and repairman. The wool card is the first essential processing
machine in our wool mill. He's single and good looking, too.

Angelique is no longer with us as she passed away on February 15,
2003 from the many effects of systemic lupus. She was a stunning beauty with
great vibrancy and had a hell-may-come attitude. It took three times plus the
effort to raise her in comparison to our other three children, as it seemed as

though she was into mischief and no matter what discipline we used, nothing worked. She was a fire storm from the beginning. Her beauty was her downfall. Boys were attracted to her like bees to honey.

There was also much to love about her. Her personality would light up a room. She expressed a kindness to others and was brave as they come. In 1984 at our farm in Raphine, Virginia, we had a major creek passing through the front of our farm. A hurricane hit us and Scott decided that it would be fun to take an inflated tire tube and boat to the raging creek. The water was so powerful that he lost control. Angelique, then ten years old, saw the picture quickly, ran down to the river, climbed a tree, and while hanging upside down on one of its limbs waited for Scott and his tube to pass. Catching Scott while flying down the creek was going to be a one-shot deal and if she missed him, he was a goner.

Without thinking of the danger to herself, Angelique, with legs hanging on a limb stretched out when Scott came by the tree, miraculously caught him and saved his life. We could never thank her enough for what she did that day. We could have lost not one, but two children. It was not meant for them to die, and Angelique's guardian angel was surely in command that rampaging day.

When she reached her teen years, boys would hide in the fields of our farm at night waiting to come to the house and get Angelique to go out with them. This occurred many times but Scott was on to it and would wake me up to go after the gathering of boys lying in wait for his sister.

Angelique succeeded once in climbing out the window and conned Jennifer into going with her. It happened that Jennifer had two of her girl friends staying with her that night and they joined what they thought would be fun and frolic with the waiting boys.

I didn't realize what occurred until about four a.m. when Scott noticed Angelique, Jennifer, and her two girlfriends were missing. We saw the "escape route" and I got into my car and tried desperately to locate the desperados. It was winter, and cold. I drove all around the town of Staunton and didn't see them. I later learned that I passed their car and Angelique ordered the girls to get down so I would not see them.

About six a.m. Angelique and her fellow unintended followers returned. Along with Diane and me, were the parents of Jennifer's girlfriends. We were all hotter than a steam iron ready to press a shirt. Jennifer spoke first. "I didn't want to go, and when I saw you Daddy, I cried and wanted to go with you. I know we did wrong."

Of course, the Angel Gabriel (aka Angelique Gabrielle) was punished severely, but grounding and other more immediate "moves" by us would prove to have a short-term effect.

At the time, I was working as an adjunct assistant professor teaching economics and law at Christendom College and had an eight-thirty morning class. I had to dress and drive one-and-a-half hours and teach in a small room with heat going full blast.

It was so hot in there that I apparently dozed off for a bit and one of the students reported me to Dean Robert Rice who was not simpatico to my early morning plight and wrote me up. This situation created an adverse, albeit mild and short range, reaction between me and the college dean. I guess Dr. Rice never knew a person like Angelique. He certainly didn't have a daughter like her.

Jennifer and Sabrina were a delight to bring up. I remember Jennifer would cry whenever I was injured. She was, and still is, so sensitive to things and has a heart of gold. On the track team in high school, she was a top runner for Buffalo Gap High School and was instrumental in the team going to the state finals one year. She was also adept with musical instruments and loved to dance. Today Jennifer is married to Jason, a fine young man, who is as hard a worker as you can find, and yes, also has a farm-boy attitude.

Sabrina is a girl with guts who can handle any problem that comes her way. She has it all in one package: brains and beauty. She too, loved music and sports in high school, and was first chair in French horn, and a great runner. For more than eight years, she has been my part-time paralegal and is now attending law school.

It is a joy to see my children grow and evolve with their dreams. What I want for them is what I want for myself, and that is to follow our dreams.

Chapter 42

Keeping On

And now as I finish reliving and telling about my fondest and most significant memories, it is truly not the end of the story. My adventures continue as my life progresses to be an exciting experience. A long time ago I decided to make my life that way. Our choices make life what we want it to be. It's certainly in our hands. The lives and stories of Vince Lombardi, General George Patton, and of course, Theodore Roosevelt are most significant to my thinking and paths I've taken, especially because of their determination to never quit. Never.

The phrase "self-made" man, or woman has been used to describe many a successful person. I believe that my own experience demonstrates the fallacy of self-made. In my life I have had a number of people who have influenced the way I would turn out. Firstly, are my parents. I was blessed with an intact family, and a father who was my personal hero. He was a quiet man, but when he spoke, people listened to the rationale and depth of wisdom he brought to light.

And then there was my mother who was determined that I would be a success so she could be proud to say I was her son. Her determination to see that happen, in Brooklyn, gave me the determination to be a success - but not in Brooklyn. Yes, I admit that I have achieved success, but only because I was able to pursue my own dreams outside of Brooklyn. Thank you, Mom and Dad!

My sister Marie and I grew up together, and as a youngster she looked up to me as her older brother. I am blessed that she has been in my life. Our mother was determined to have at least one child grow up and stay near her in Brooklyn even though Marie fought our mother's persuasion. Marie kept true to her own authenticity by having her farm in Mom's back yard with beautiful flowers and wonderful vegetables. She learned to be a great cook. She now lives out on Long Island. Thank you, Marie!

My godmother, Elma and her mother, Rose Senatore, were so influential in my religious upbringing. Those two gave me the foundation and the spiritual stability that when life threw me its curves, my religious strength carried me through. I had direction and strength that they instilled in me. Thank you, Elma and Rose!

In education, it was the religious sisters and brothers, priests, deacons and yes, bishops that educated me and saw in me the potential to be somebody. Thank you all!

My wife, Diane, who has put up with me for almost forty-five years, was and is my brakes slowing me down and awaking me to reality. Diane offered to our conversations, "Suppose this or that would happen.." She shows me the potential downsides to many of my endeavors, but has never stopped me even when difficulties arose. Even if she disagreed with my ideas, my loving wife has been a steadfast, supportive and helpful partner in life. Thank you, Diane!

The future is there because of my four children. Francis Scott Cestari is available morning, noon, and night to get things done on the farm, in the wool mill and in the house. A soft-spoken man, his ideas are many times better than mine. He takes on jobs and sees them through to the finish. What a wonderful son.

Angelique's joyful spirit is still around even though she went to our Lord several years ago. The Pumpkin Fest will always remind me of her for she gave the festival its name, and helped to plan it. Her two children, Caleb and Ethan, are constant reminders of Angelique and our family enjoys seeing them frequently.

Jennifer, a sweet, beautiful child has been involved in our wool business in the past and is still there when we need her. She helps with sales at festivals, even though she works full time as a legal secretary for a fine law firm in Staunton, and is also working towards her master's degree. I hope that our business will grow to the extent that she could again be a full participant in the wool business since she has a natural aptitude for fashion and sales.

And Sabrina, who has a quick analytical mind, can do most anything she puts her mind to do. In addition to a lovely personality, she can care for, shear, and trim the hooves of sheep. She has earned her bachelors and masters degrees, has now completed her first year at Ave Maria Law School in Naples, Florida, while as a single mother caring and raising her children, Tristan and India Rose.

Thank you to all my children, along with your mother, for enriching my life!

Am I a self-made man? I hope that my life experiences will inspire you and, in turn, you will inspire others to look on life with joy each and every day of your life.

God bless you and yours!